D0779412

RELIGION

Key Concepts in Philosophy

Key Concepts in Philosophy

Series Editors: John Mullarkey (University of Dundee) and
Caroline Williams (Queen Mary, University of London)

Religion

Key Concepts in Philosophy

Brendan Sweetman

continuum

Continuum
The Tower Building
11 York Road
London SE1 7NX

80 Maiden Lane
Suite 704
New York
NY 10038

© Brendan Sweetman 2007

All rights reserved. No part of this publication may be reproduced or
transmitted in any form or by any means, electronic or mechanical,
including photocopying, recording, or any information storage or retrieval
system, without prior permission in writing from the publishers.

British Library Cataloguing-in-Publication Data
A catalogue record for this book is available from the British Library.

ISBN: 0-8264-8626-6 (hardback)   9780826486264
0-8264-8627-4 (paperback)   9780826486271

Library of Congress Cataloguing-in-Publication Data
A catalog record for this book is available from the Library of Congress.

Typeset by Servis Filmsetting Ltd, Manchester
Printed and bound in Great Britain by
MPG Books Ltd, Bodmin, Cornwall

For Curtis Hancock

CONTENTS

CHAPTER 1

INTRODUCTION: THE GOD QUESTION

Religion is a quite fascinating subject, as even those who are not religious will agree. It evokes the realm of the transcendent that seems to call out to all of us because we are finite human beings; it reaches out to the infinite, and offers a way to make sense out of the various mysteries of human existence. Belief in God (or a Supreme Reality) and the afterlife is generally a major part of the religious worldview, as is prayer, various ritualistic practices and a specific account of morality. Moreover, the religious worldview, in its various forms, has been incredibly influential in history. The vast majority of people who have ever lived were and are religious believers, and religious views have, at least up until recently, decisively shaped our approach to morality and society, law and politics. The religious understanding of the world, and of human life, has been the dominant one in history. Many people have found it to be an extremely profound, satisfying and fulfilling philosophy of life, despite the various problems, mistakes, sins and abuses all too evident throughout the history of religion.

Yet religion has often come in for criticism from various quarters, both in the past but especially in the contemporary world. These criticisms are of two sorts. First, criticisms of specific beliefs, doctrines or teachings of particular religions, such as criticism of the Catholic Church's position on women priests, or on the emphasis in Protestantism on the centrality of the Bible. But, second, there are also more fundamental criticisms. Some have argued that the religious view of the world in general is not rational, that no reasonable, educated, enlightened person, in the modern world especially, should subscribe to this worldview, support it publicly, or try to influence society in accordance with it. This particular criticism is founded on the claim that there is no God, and so all religions, no matter how old or how influential they may be, are in some sense fundamentally misguided. And since there is no God, most of the doctrinal beliefs of most religions would also be wrong in an important sense. Religion, this argument continues, may have practical value as a way of providing comfort for people, perhaps as a way of coping with reality, or as a way of organizing and motivating people to do good, but it is not based on factual truth, and is perhaps even dangerous for humanity in the long run. This second type of criticism – that the religious worldview in general is misguided – is one of our main concerns in this book, as we explore the main questions, issues and themes involved in any philosophical examination of religious belief.

This modern critical approach has put today's religious believer on the defensive, despite the fact that the overwhelming majority of people remain religious believers. Yet there is a tendency today to question a person's religious beliefs in a way that perhaps one would not question the beliefs of a secularist or a Marxist, for example. One might disagree with a secularist or a Marxist, of course, not just on one or two issues, but in the sense of rejecting that complete worldview, but one still does not quite think of this in terms of saying that the secularist or Marxist worldview is not rational: that no reasonable person should hold a secularist worldview, that this worldview is irrational superstition and is not worthy of having influence in society. But this is how more and more people in the modern world look upon religious belief. No doubt for some this attitude is not well thought out, is due to peer pressure, or perhaps is motivated by cultural context, and so for all these reasons might be dismissed. Nevertheless, there is a tendency in today's world to put a question mark over the religious worldview in a way that puts the religious believer on the defensive, whereas in most of history it is true to say that he was on the offensive! We might see this tendency represented in a number of ways: a religious believer might be reluctant to refer to his religious beliefs in the public discussion of a profound moral question; mainstream media outlets might routinely ignore the religious approach when discussing the questions of the day; governments might discourage religious input into debates over their various policies; religious beliefs and values may have less overall influence in people's day-to-day lives than they once did.

All of this brings to the forefront the question of the rationality of religious belief: in particular, the rationality of belief in God and of the religious worldview and also the question of how the rationality of religious belief compares with the rationality of other worldviews that compete with it, especially secularism. The aim of this book is to explore these matters from the point of view of what philosophers have to say about them, and in so doing to explore the myriad related questions and issues involved in any discussion of the key concepts of religious belief.

IS YOUR WORLDVIEW REASONABLE?

Most people who are reading this book are probably religious believers. And some no doubt are atheists or secularists. A question I would like you to think about in this section, whether you are a religious believer or an atheist, is one that we sometimes overlook because of the pressures of modern life: is your worldview reasonable? Is the worldview to which you subscribe, and perhaps to which your family subscribes, or which you rear your family in – that worldview, in short, by which you regulate your beliefs, values and behavior – is that worldview a reasonable worldview? And, just as important, how would you defend it, or argue for it, if called upon to do so by someone who rejected it as irrational?

This is a question which members of *every* worldview should be concerned about. It is also a question which religious believers, in particular, have often tended to downplay or even ignore. Religious believers have sometimes been more concerned with living their worldview, and with promoting it, than with thinking about its reasonableness, or how it might compare to other worldviews in terms of its overall rationality. But philosophers of religion generally insist that one *should* be concerned with the rationality of one's worldview, that this matter is of major significance, especially if one is going to live in accordance with that worldview and propose that others do so too, at least in part. It is not necessary, of course, that every member of a particular religion should be able to defend their worldview in a sophisticated philosophical or theological way. That would be an unrealistic expectation. Most people have neither the time nor the training nor the confidence to take on this task. But it is necessary that *someone* in a particular religious tradition – the philosophers, intellectuals and any other interested persons – should be able to make some attempt at explaining why that particular worldview is reasonable.

I like to illustrate this point by the example of the Abominable Snowman Worship Society, a society that worships the Abominable Snowman. The members of this society want you to join the group and can give you a special deal, because, following good western business practices, you have come along during recruitment week, when an eye-catching discount is on offer! But when you attend your first (exploratory) meeting of the Society, you will most likely want to know why members worship the Abominable Snowman. But suppose that nobody in the group can address this question, that nobody has ever really considered it, that nobody is even interested in it, and, to come right down to it, they don't particularly want anyone in the group who raises this question! All of this would leave you wondering if belief in and worship of the Abominable Snowman is rational. And you would most likely decline the invitation to join the group: it is the same, I contend, with *any* worldview. The question of its rationality is essential to whether people should accept the view, should practise it, should see it as respectable when compared with other worldviews, and as to whether one is entitled to make contributions to public debates based on the worldview. It is necessary that somebody in each worldview be concerned with the rationality of the worldview, should pay serious attention to the reasons and evidence to support the worldview, even if most do not. And those that do pay attention to this matter can help articulate and defend the worldview for the benefit of other members of the worldview, as well as for outsiders.

SOME TERMINOLOGY

Before we get going on the main questions of the book, it will be helpful to clarify some key terms and concepts, so that we are clear on what is being talked about. My approach to the task of exploring the key concepts of religious belief is based around a consideration of the question, just mentioned, as to whether *the religious view of the world* is reasonable or not. But what do we mean by the religious view of the world? Our answer to this question will also serve as our definition of religion. Religion has been defined in many ways, and many of the definitions overlap, as we might expect. Some thinkers offer a broad definition, others a more restrictive one. American theologian Vergilius Ferm defined religion in this way: 'To be religious is to effect in some way . . . a vital adjustment to whatever is reacted to or regarded implicitly or explicitly as worthy of serious and ulterior concern.' The American philosopher William James drew attention to a moral dimension when he defined religion as 'the belief there is an unseen order, and that our supreme good lies in harmoniously adjusting ourselves thereto'. Ninian Smart gives a more elaborate definition: religion is 'a set of institutionalized rituals with a tradition and expressing and/or evoking sacral sentiments directed at a divine or trans-divine focus seen in the context of the human phenomeno-logical environment and at least partially described by myths or by myths and doctrines'.[1] It is obvious that it is hard to get a definition that will do the job, that will capture all of the salient features unique to the religious worldview. But these are interesting definitions that give us a sense of the features we need to capture in a general working definition of religion.

Our definition needs only to capture the main points about the religious view of reality; we do not need an exhaustive definition that would cover every type of religion and religious activity. Thus, *religion* may be understood as a (usually) complex system of beliefs (about reality, the human person and morality), that are life-regulating (they influence how we live), that are expressed in certain types of rituals and practices, and that are based in large part on a belief in a sacred, transcendent (unseen) reality. There is usually a belief in God, or at least in a Supreme Being of some kind who is the creator of all life, and also a belief in an afterlife that is signifi-cantly better than this life and that is often our ultimate destiny. Religions also generally hold that human beings consist of body and soul, and that two of our most significant qualities are our intellect (reasoning ability) and our free will (we are moral agents). Most religions also accept that one can communicate with God through prayer. This is what I will mean by religion, or the religious worldview, in this book.

My main aim is to discuss the questions that typically come up about the reasonableness of this way of looking at reality. I am not as interested in investigating specific doctrinal or moral differences between various religious denominations, though I will discuss some of these in the chapter on religious pluralism. But, in general, I want to investigate some basic philosophical questions about reli-gious belief: does God exist?; what is God's nature?; why does God allow evil?; what is a religious experience?; are religion and science compatible or are they essentially in conflict (as some believe)?; is the scientific theory of evolution evidence against the existence of God?; what are we to make of the fact that there are many different religions in the world? These are the main questions that philosophers ask about religion. After one has formulated an approach to answering them, one can then begin to think philosophically about specific matters of doctrine, and of the various differences and disagreements between specific religious denominations. But that latter task is not the task of this book.

I will approach these questions mainly from the point of view of classical theism. *Classical theism* is the traditional view of God found in most western religions, and some eastern religions too. It dates back at least to Plato and Aristotle and was totally dominant in the Middle Ages, right up to modern times. It holds that God exists as a transcendent being, over and above the world; that God is all-knowing, all-powerful and all-good; that God created the world and all life according to a particular plan; that everything that exists depends on God; and that God cannot change, among other significant beliefs. The religions of Judaism, Christianity and Islam have generally held this view of God. Classical theism is *monotheistic*, which means that its proponents hold that there is only one God. This has been the main view in western culture, with *polytheism*, the view that there are several Gods, more popular in the east. In our discussions in this book, we will initially approach the various questions we are considering – such as whether God exists – from the point of view of classical theism and monotheism, but we will examine other approaches along the way as well (especially in the chapter on the nature of God, where we will explore various views of God in detail). As noted above, I wish to emphasize more general questions that philosophers ask about religion, especially the principal ones: does God exist? and is religious belief in general a rational worldview? Philosophers are more interested in asking whether the general religious view of the world is reasonable or not, rather than in examining specific doctrinal disputes between religions (though this has been changing a bit in recent times). I will approach the questions of the book mainly from a western perspective, since that is the perspective I am most familiar with and most comfortable with, and is probably the perspective of most readers. Nevertheless, the eastern perspective, especially where it is different and distinctive, will not be ignored and I will refer to it from time to time.

As we ask questions aimed at probing the religious worldview, it will also be helpful to keep before our minds, in a general sense, that worldview which is today most critical of religious belief, the world-view of *secularism*. It is true to say that secularism is now a major worldview in modern culture and is a major player in social, moral and political issues, and in the cultural debate shaping the future direction of society. *Secularism* is the view that all of reality is phys-ical in nature, consisting of some configuration of matter and energy, and that science is the key to understanding all of reality (this view is also sometimes called *naturalism* by philosophers). In the latter half of the twentieth century, this view came to be offered as a positive thesis. This means that the secularist does not start out saying that there is no God; rather, he or she starts with these posi-tive claims about reality, and the view that there is no God, soul, or afterlife are consequences of these claims, or follow from them. Secularists hold that the universe, and all life on earth, including human life, are random occurrences. They also believe that we need secular accounts of morality and politics, and that the secularist worldview should be the main influence on society as we move into the twenty-first century. For the purposes of the general debate between religion and secularism, we need also to regard secularism as a general way of looking at the world, while recognizing that there are many different kinds of secularism, each with its own propo-nents, themes and emphases.

By identifying the secularist worldview up front, I want to draw attention to the key point that many of the issues in the philosophy of religion must now be understood *against a background* of the debate between the religious worldview and the secularist worldview. This is because if the religious view turns out not to be true, or not to be reasonable, *some other view* must be true or more reasonable, and this is usually supposed to be the secularist view. So any critique offered of the religious worldview today must increasingly be taken to mean that the secularist view is the *correct* view. This means that we need to keep secularist claims and arguments in mind even as we debate the rationality of religious belief. This is also a crucial matter when we are considering the rationality of our worldview and how it stacks up against other worldviews that are competing with ours in the *political* realm in a pluralist society.

Before concluding this section there are several concepts that it will be helpful to clarify. The term *theist* is a term many philosophers of religion use to describe someone who believes in God (from the Greek word for God, *theos*). *Philosophy of religion* may be defined as the attempt by philosophers to investigate the rationality of basic religious claims. Philosophers of religion are usually, but not always, religious believers themselves. This is why philosophy of religion differs from *apologetics*, which may be understood as the attempt to defend the claims of a particular religion, including its doctrinal claims, against intellectual objections presented by outsiders. Obviously there is some overlap, but one way to keep them distinct is to remember that a philosopher of religion could be an atheist, but an apologist for a particular religion would not normally be an atheist. Nor is philosophy of religion the same as theology. *Theology* is a discipline that generally *assumes* the reasonableness of a particular religious tradition and perhaps the reliability of certain religious texts. Evangelical theologians, for example, would assume that the Christian worldview is reasonable and that the Bible is an authoritative religious text, and would work within this framework. Philosophy of religion, on the other hand, tries to take nothing for granted (especially nothing controversial) at the beginning of the inquiry. It tries to approach the key questions of religion with a blank slate, as it were, to see what can be achieved in thinking about these questions by philosophical reasoning alone.

It is also helpful to distinguish between various forms of atheism. My old literature professor used to make a distinction between a church atheist and a God atheist. A *church atheist* is a person who, when asked, would say that he does not believe in God, but upon further examination, it turns out that his real problem is with his church. He might express this by saying things like: 'well, I don't like the moral code of my religion', or 'I can't stand the bishops', or 'don't talk to me about religion!' He has not quite made clear in his own mind the distinction between rejecting belief in God and rejecting or being dissatisfied with his own particular religious denomination, a distinction we all recognize in theory, but often forget at the level of religious practice. This type of atheist is to be distinguished from a God atheist. A *God atheist* is someone who genuinely does not believe in God, who does not think that God exists. She is not making the mistake of confusing dissatisfaction with her particular church with disbelieving in God. Many people who sound like God atheists are probably really church atheists (especially those who have lapsed from the religion of their birth), even if they don't realize it. Our concern in this book is not with church atheism but with God atheism.

This brings us to an important distinction between *negative atheism* and *positive atheism*, a distinction that ties in with our discussion of secularism and naturalism above. Up until the twentieth century, atheism was almost always presented as a negative thesis or position. It was negative in three ways. First, the atheist defined his view in terms of what it was not, rather than in terms of what it was. So in the past an atheist might say, when asked what he believed, that he did not think that God existed, or that he rejected religious morality, or that he did not follow his church's teachings, all claims about what he doesn't believe, not about what he does believe. Second, he often regarded himself negatively from a psychological point of view, because he was usually in the minority, and perhaps couldn't avoid understanding his identity in terms of *what he was not* (a religious believer) rather than in terms of what he was (an atheist)! Third – and this is the most important – the atheist also *defended* his view negatively, by attacking religion and arguments for religious belief. He did this rather than presenting positive arguments in favour of atheism.

However, in the twentieth century all of this changed, and this marks the general transition from negative atheism to *positive atheism* (or secularism). Atheists realized that a more cultivated approach was necessary. They were originally like scientists who defended the Big Bang theory of the origin of the universe by constantly attacking the steady-state theory of the origin of the universe. Eventually, these scientists had to decide what they believed about the origin of the universe (in a positive sense), and had to start defending the Big Bang theory with positive evidence and not just by attacking its rivals. Nowadays, a secularist is much more likely to present secularism as a positive thesis, one that identifies what he believes, rather than what he does not believe. As noted above, secularists will say they believe that human life is the outcome of a purely random, naturalistic process (evolution), and that all reality is physical. And, very important, their defence of these claims will not now consist simply of attacking the arguments for religious belief: they will try to offer positive arguments to support these views. Where will they get these arguments? Like many thinkers struggling to articulate a position, they will turn to whatever is available at the time to help them with their arguments, and many of them have turned to modern science, especially to evolution, genetics and neurology. All of this has created the impression in much of popular culture that modern science is really on the side of atheism. This is not true and it is an issue that we will come back to in several of the discussions that follow.

FAITH AND REASON

It is very common in the United States, but less so in other countries, to use the term 'faith' to describe religious belief. But this term can be quite misleading. The word 'faith' has unfortunate connotations, especially today, and can be used to set up a somewhat artificial distinction between faith on the one hand and reason on the other. The term frequently carries with it the connotation that religious beliefs are outside reason, or that religious believers are not interested in the rationality of their views, or worst of all, that religious beliefs are not even reasonable. This is often how secularists might use the term, but it is also sometimes used this way by religious believers themselves.

The most important sense of the term from the point of view of philosophy of religion is the cognitive or propositional sense which refers to holding a belief for which the evidence is less than 100 per cent certain or decisive. Religious beliefs involve propositions about God, about God's relationship to the world and human beings, and about morality, among many other propositions. The religious believer cannot prove these propositions to be true in the sense of giving a scientific proof, or presenting decisive evidence for them. But he can at least try to show that they are *rational* to believe. This is the most appropriate use of the term 'faith' in philosophy of religion and marks the best understanding of the relationship between faith and reason. A religious believer holds many things on faith, but he hopes that it is a *rational faith* (not an irrational faith), and the work of philosophy of religion is, among other things, an attempt to investigate the rationality of religious belief.

On this understanding of the term 'faith', it is the case that all worldviews – religious or secularist – involve faith in this cognitive sense. That is to say, all worldviews hold beliefs about the nature of reality, the nature of the human person and the nature of morality, to which the adherents of the worldview pledge their commitment, but which they cannot prove decisively. Although it may be possible to back up some of these beliefs with rational arguments and evidence, it is still necessary to *commit* to them, since any arguments we have will fall short of proof, because of the subject matter involved. The subject matter of worldviews, which involves the three subjects mentioned, does not admit of scientific proof. This is true for all worldviews, secularist ones as well as religious ones. So if one accepts various beliefs about the nature of reality, or the human person, or morality, this acceptance will involve a commitment to these beliefs: *a movement of the will* as well as of the intellect. So, in fact, a religious believer and a secularist are in the same boat in this respect, a point frequently overlooked. We are often inclined simply to accept it as true without giving much thought to the matter that it is only religious belief that involves faith, but not secularism. But now that secularism is a positive worldview in itself, and a major cultural player to boot, it is no longer appropriate to overlook the fact that it is a worldview with many controversial beliefs that are the subject of contentious debate, and that its adherents accept many of these beliefs at least partially *on faith*.

Indeed, perhaps we need a broader definition of philosophy of religion for the modern world. It may no longer be appropriate to see it as simply a sub-discipline which investigates only the rationality of religious belief. This is because there is a sense in which to investigate this question today is also *automatically to investigate the rationality of secularism*. Once one recognizes that secularism is now a positive worldview, in the sense described above, with its positive theses and arguments, it seems to change our understanding of what philosophy of religion involves. When one asks, for example, whether it is rational to believe in God, one is also automatically asking whether it is rational not to believe in God – and this is simply to ask whether it is rational to believe that all of reality is physical, a foundational belief of secularism. This confirms my point above that most of the fascinating issues today must be debated against a *background* of the debate over the rationality of secularism vs. the rationality of religious belief, not just against a background of whether the religious believer is reasonable or not!

Medieval philosopher St Anselm said that his motive in probing the rationality of religious belief was *fides quaerens intellectum*, faith seeking understanding. Anselm and other philosophers recognized that while there is a degree of faith involved in committing to religious claims, the reasonableness of these claims is still important and the intelligent, philosophically minded believer should address this matter. These philosophers were not content to hold the view that since their religious beliefs were a matter of faith there was no need or no room for a rational discussion of them. They were, therefore, very committed to the discipline of philosophy as a way of questioning, clarifying and supporting the main beliefs and concepts of the religious worldview. And so Christian thinkers like Thomas Aquinas extended this way of thinking to include studying the views of scholars from other cultures, many of whom were not Christian, as well as to the study of science. Medieval and later religious philosophers were much impressed by Augustine's point that 'all truth is one', the view that many areas of study, including science, can discover truths concerning various areas of life and that religious belief, if it is to be rationally grounded, must seek to welcome and accommodate these truths. If a claim is established as true in one discipline, Augustine said, it must be true in all disciplines. This approach defines the approach of philosophy of religion today and it will be the approach in this book.

So, with these introductory points in mind, in what follows we will work through many of the stimulating questions that are the subject matter of philosophy of religion. We shall do so in the company of the work of outstanding thinkers, both past and present, who have contributed to our understanding of these matters. My aim is to acquaint readers with the main issues and the main lines of debate relating to the various questions in a way that is balanced, fair and historically informed. My own views – I am a theist in the Catholic tradition – will occasionally come to the surface, of course, but my aim is to present the strongest arguments on both sides of the debate in such a way that the reader will get an overall understanding of the topic, will be challenged by the philosophical questions and will be able to make informed judgements. The book is aimed at the student and the general reader interested in learning more about what philosophers have to say about religion. No previous knowledge of philosophy is assumed or necessary. I have also avoided using specialized philosophical vocabulary or technical jargon. Further reading can be found in the notes at the end of the book and in the bibliography.

My hope for readers, especially students, is that during this journey they will be stimulated to think through for themselves the great questions of religious belief, and that they will be inspired to seek an approach that is philosophically rigorous as well as historically informed. My hope also is that readers will be gripped by the wonder that gives rise to both philosophical and religious questions, a wonder that so many have experienced who have grappled with arguably the most interesting questions of all.

A number of people helped me as I worked on this book. I am very grateful in particular to Brian Davies, Edward Furton, Douglas Geivett and Curtis Hancock. I am also grateful to the staff at Continuum Books, and to the editors of the Key Concepts in Philosophy series, for their support and hard work. Finally, I wish to thank my family most of all for all their help and encouragement while I worked on this project. Without their great support and companionship, this book would not have been possible.

CHAPTER 2

FIRST CAUSE AND DESIGN

This universe that we all call home is an awe-inspiring place. Most of us take its existence for granted and don't pause often enough to consider its remarkable size and complexity. The universe consists of galaxies (ours is called the Milky Way, and a near neighbour is Andromeda); each galaxy is thousands of light years across; and there are estimated to be a hundred billion galaxies with a billion trillion stars. When one considers these facts, as well as the nature of space-time, the organization of the planets, the nature of life, the existence of rationality, the existence of morality, the nature of mathematics and the existence of spirituality, it is hard not to be impressed, indeed almost overwhelmed, by the enormity, majesty and mystery of our universe. This is true no matter what one's worldview is. Pondering on the existence and nature of the universe rarely fails to provoke wonder, awe and curiosity in the minds of human beings. Indeed, if one spends any time at all reflecting on the kind of universe we live in, one almost cannot fail to begin thinking about two broad questions. First, how did our universe get here, where did it come from, did it have a cause, what is the cause? Second, is the universe designed, does it have a purpose, why is it here, is there a reason it is the way it is? And it is no wonder that arguments dealing with these two questions have been among the most important arguments considered by philosophers for the existence of God, or a Supreme Being.

In this chapter, I will attempt to provide an overview of two of the main arguments offered by religious philosophers for the existence of God – the cosmological argument and the teleological argument. The cosmological argument, more popularly known as the first cause argument (from the Greek work, *cosmos*, meaning 'world'), and the teleological argument, more popularly known as the argument from design (from the Greek word, *telos*, meaning 'purpose'), are part of natural theology. The sub-discipline of natural theology within philosophy of religion involves examining any evidence for the existence of God that can be found in the physical universe (including from the study of life), and then attempting to draw some conclusion about whether or not God's existence can be inferred on the basis of the evidence found. Natural theology has often reached a positive conclusion on this matter. It is a distinctly philosophical enterprise and, despite its name, should not be confused with the discipline of theology, though it obviously would have implications for theology if the project was generally successful.

Although natural theology has been practised since the dawn of man, there is sometimes a debate about what its aim should be. Is it necessary to *prove* the existence of God, or would it be sufficient to show that belief in God is *reasonable*, given the evidence of the physical world? My own view is that the aim of natural theology should be to show that belief in God is reasonable and perhaps, if possible, more reasonable than the alternatives, as I hinted in our introductory chapter. The subject matter of worldviews, as I noted then, is such that it is not likely that we can offer scientific-type proofs regarding the main beliefs of our worldview, religious or secularist. But it is necessary to try to show that our beliefs are at least reasonable, and it would be a good day's work for the natural theologian if he or she could show that religious belief is reasonable. Some natural theologians will occasionally go further, of course, and claim that natural theology can prove the existence of God, irrespective of whether it actually needs to or not, though it is fair to say that this is a minority view today. Arguments for the existence of God are still regularly referred to as 'proofs', but usually with the understanding that something less than what is sometimes called a 'knock-down' proof is offered. Let us turn first to consider some different versions of the cosmological argument, which, although they all adopt the same basic approach, have important differences.

THE KALĀM COSMOLOGICAL ARGUMENT

St Bonaventure (1221–1274) was a contemporary of St Thomas Aquinas (1224–1274), and they often argued back and forth on natural theology. They shared the same approach to the question of

God's existence, but differed on how to develop the argument. We will look at Bonaventure's approach in this section, especially as it has been developed and modernized by influential modern philosopher of religion William Lane Craig. We will come back to St Thomas's version of the argument in the next section. The argument excited much interest in the Middle Ages among a group of philosophers who are part of the kalām tradition in Islamic philosophy, and so it has come to be known as the 'kalām argument' (kalām is Arabic for 'speech').[1]

Bonaventure, and those who share his basic approach, begin by taking any event in the physical world, say the Amazon river, and asking how it was caused. It is important to specify that they are not seeking what philosophers sometimes call the *local* cause of the Amazon river, but the *ultimate* cause. The local cause might be that the Ice Age produced water and rain that carved out the Amazon river bed, supplied it with water, and was responsible for joining it up with the ocean. This is the kind of cause that science in its everyday practice would seek. But the philosopher wants to know the ultimate cause, the deeper cause, of the Amazon river, how the Amazon river got there in the first place. This is a much more difficult question, of course, yet it is a perfectly reasonable question for a curious human being to ask, perhaps a human being who is beginning to think about the universe in a deeper way. One obvious way to seek out the ultimate cause is to consider some of the prior causes that led to the Amazon river as an end result. Thus, we might say that falling temperatures on a large scale over most of the earth's surface caused the Ice Age. And that these low temperatures were caused by strong winds sweeping over the earth. And the winds were caused by gases in the earth's atmosphere; the gases were caused by changes in the earth's orbit around the sun, and so on. What we have going now is a chain of causes, stretching back into the past, each one causing the succeeding one, and bringing us up to the present group of events that make up the universe, including the Amazon river. So far, so good.

However, eventually we will have to deal with another question about the chain of explanatory causes: does it go on forever into the past, or did it have a beginning? Was there a first event in the chain of causes? These are the only possibilities from a logical point of view. We can speculate about other possibilities, such as the view that time goes in a loop, or that there are many universes, but these seem to be little more than (metaphysical) speculations. The defender of this form of the cosmological argument holds that it is reasonable not to spend too much time on alternatives that are not consistent with current scientific evidence. The only plausible, reasonable options on the table for how the chain of events began is either that there is a first event, or that the universe has an infinite past.

Bonaventure's version of the cosmological argument gets its distinctiveness at this point, because he famously argued that the universe *cannot* have an infinite past, and so must have a beginning, a first event.[2] This argument has been developed in an interesting and provocative way in recent times by William Lane Craig.[3] Craig's arguments are intriguing and have generated much discussion. He believes that the universe must have had a beginning – a first event – and that this conclusion can be supported on both philosophical and scientific grounds. Let us take the scientific grounds first since they are likely to be more familiar to us, at least in broad outline, and so need not delay us too much in the exposition of the argument.

According to Craig, a good natural theologian should be familiar with the main arguments of the latest scientific theories, especially as they might have a bearing on religious questions. He subscribes to Augustine's view, noted in the Introduction, that 'all truth is one'; and so one should not be afraid to appeal to scientific evidence if it is relevant to one's arguments. The current main theory concerning the origin of the universe, accepted by the vast majority of scientists today, is the Big Bang theory. The Big Bang theory says that the universe began between ten and twenty billion years ago in a huge explosion. This explosion, called a singularity, consisted of a point of infinitely dense and infinitely hot matter. The debris of the explosion contained all the seeds of everything in our universe. The Big Bang theory shows that the universe had a beginning in time. It would have been the first event in our universe. The theory is well confirmed, and represents good scientific evidence that the universe had a beginning. It shows that there was a first event, and therefore that history (and time) has a finite past.[4]

There is a second scientific theory that appears to confirm the conclusion that the universe had a beginning. This is the evidence from the second law of thermodynamics. This law says that the entropy in the universe tends to a maximum. Entropy is the measure of total disorder or chaos in a system. What this means in practical terms is that in a closed system, processes will eventually run down and die, given enough time. A closed system is a system which contains everything in it that exists, and which has nothing outside it. The universe is such a system, and the eventual running down of the universe is called the 'heat death' of the universe. Now the question is, according to Craig, why has the universe not experienced this heat death yet? The obvious answer is that the heat death of the universe would take about x billion years, and so far only less than x billion years have elapsed. Craig's point, however, is that this answer is not acceptable if one believes that the universe has an infinite past. This is because we would already *have had* an infinite amount of time elapse before the present moment, and that should be more than enough time for the heat death to occur. The second law of thermodynamics, like the Big Bang theory, therefore supports the view that the universe had a beginning.

These considerations lead Craig to argue for a stronger claim. This is that the notion of an actual infinity does not make any logical sense, and that there could be no such thing in the real world. He does not deny that the concept of infinity is useful in mathematics and set theory, but these disciplines involve only potential infinities, infinities that exist in the mind only. An infinity is only represented in mathematics, for example, and is never real, never actually exists. But if we claim that the universe has an infinite past, we would be saying that an actual infinite series of physical events really exists, and Craig argues that this is not possible. To show this, Craig attempts to generate a series of logical paradoxes that would result if we operated with the assumption that an actual infinity really existed. The first example he takes involves a library with an infinite number of books, where the books are stacked on the shelves in alternate colours, red, black, red, black, and so on. The library would have an infinite number of red books and an infinite number of black books, and an infinite number of total books. It would have, in short, the same amount of books in total as it had in a single colour. In addition, if one were to take some books out of the library, an infinite number would still remain, and if one were to add any books to the library, the overall total would still be an infinite number. His point is that when we start trying to imagine what would have to be the case for an actual infinite series of physical events to really exist out there in the real world, we begin to see that the notion generates several serious puzzles and simply does not make sense. This example leads to logical absurdities and suggests that the notion of an actual infinite series of physical events is not intelligible. Craig also refers to an example where the earth and Jupiter are orbiting the sun from eternity, but the earth is orbiting at three times the speed of Jupiter. Yet if they have been orbiting from eternity, they will have completed the *same* number of orbits, but again this seems absurd.

Craig has a second line of argument for the same conclusion. In this particular way of looking at the matter, he relies on the notion of the logical impossibility of counting to, or of crossing, an infinity. Simplifying the argument a little, it goes like this: if there were an infinite number of days before today, then today would never arrive. (Because it is impossible to cross an infinity). But today has arrived. Therefore, the number of days before today must have been finite. We can appreciate this argument better perhaps if we imagine ourselves standing far off in the past, with the assumption that the past is infinite, and looking towards the future. The question is not how do we get from point A to point B. The answer to this question is easy, and involves a finite amount of days. But if we ask how did we ever get to point B at all, and if the answer is supposed to be that we crossed an infinity of events, this is absurd. The same problem applies to point A as well, of course, or to *any* point in history one cares to take.

There have been a number of interesting objections to Craig's reasoning. A common reply to his arguments is to say that even if the universe is infinite, we don't need to worry about it too much because, from any particular point one takes in history, there is always a finite time between that point and some future point, so we can avoid the logical absurdities.[5] From this point of view, an infinite regress might look plausible. Craig's response, as we have seen, is that this is not a satisfactory answer for philosophers seeking the ultimate cause of things. This is because philosophers are asking how we (ultimately) got to any particular point in history, and if the answer is supposed to be that we crossed an infinite amount of time, this is deeply problematic, and so, since *that point* in history occurred, the answer must be that we crossed a *finite* amount of time. To give an explanation for the cause of any particular event in history is fine as far as it goes, but it does not answer the question of why there are particular events in history at all. A second objection has been raised by Paul Draper.[6] He argues that the logical paradoxes and absurdities generated by Craig's examples only seem to work if one *assumes* that the concept of an actual infinity is absurd. Perhaps if we took the concept more seriously, Draper argues, we would have to look at things differently, perhaps accepting that a library could have the same number of books in a single colour as it has in the whole collection. The onus of proof, though, for this line of argument is surely on Draper, and more work needs to be done to show that an actual infinity makes logical sense.

Third, Quentin Smith had argued that Craig's library examples do not generate the paradoxes he thinks they generate. Smith believes that one could add to an actual infinite number of books if we take 'any infinite collection of existing items, say, of books, and match them one-to-one with all positive whole numbers . . .'; this is an actual infinite, Smith holds, because 'the books really exist and there is an actually infinite number of numbers in the series . . .'[7] This argument seems right, but Craig believes it begs the question because it does not really start with an actual infinite. If one starts with an actual infinite, Craig replies, one cannot add to the system because 'an actual infinity of objects already exists that completely exhausts the natural number system – every possible number has been instantiated in reality on the spine of a book'.[8] This is what an actual infinity is, and Craig believes that many arguments, like Smith's, miss this point in their objections. They are still treating an actual infinity as if it were only a potential infinity.

A more general objection to the argument, one often raised by students of science, is that the law of conservation of energy is a possible objection to the view that an actual infinity cannot exist. The law of conservation of energy in fact constitutes the first law of thermodynamics. The law states that any collection of objects isolated from the rest of the universe can neither gain not lose total energy, no matter how the objects interact with each other in their environment. In this sense, energy can neither be created nor destroyed. The sum total of energy in any closed system always remains the same (or is conserved). It can be converted into different forms – say from chemical energy into mechanical energy – but the amount of energy is the same, and no energy is destroyed. Does this law not show that energy is infinite? While this law is well established and very useful in science, it does not show that energy is infinite in the sense that it has always existed. So in this key sense the existence of energy would not constitute an example of an actual infinite. For the purposes of our discussion here, the law, more properly stated, says that when energy *comes into existence*, it can never be created or destroyed. But stated this way the law of conservation of energy cannot serve as a critique of the cosmological argument, for it does not argue that energy has always existed, nor does it provide an explanation of how energy came into existence in the first place.

After establishing that the universe has a beginning, the next step in Craig's argument is to ask the question, not what might have caused the first event (this question comes later), but *did the first event have a cause*? This is a subtle, but vitally important, logical step in the overall argument. With this step, he is trying to draw attention to the fact that if we are to be reasonable, we *must* conclude that the first event has a cause. This is the only possible answer to this question for a rational person. Of course, the Big Bang is a unique event, being the first event, and so it is clear that the question Craig is asking cannot be answered by science. This is because we are dealing with the first event in the universe, so we cannot give our usual answer to the question of the cause of an event, which would involve invoking an earlier physical (local) cause. This is a logical conclusion which applies no matter what the first event turns out to be. If we discover in the future that the Big Bang was not the first event, but that there was a *prior* first event, the Little Bang, which caused the Big Bang, then our question in this part of the argument needs to be asked of the Little Bang. What is obvious at this point, according to supporters of this version of the argument, is that no scientific answer to this question is possible. We have only two alternatives here, Craig believes. The first is to say that the first event must have a cause, even though we can see no way that it could be a physical cause open to investigation by the domain of science. The second is to say that the first event *has no cause*. But this second answer is not reasonable. Which is more reasonable, Craig asks: that the first event had a cause, or that it came into existence without a cause, just appeared, as it were, just 'popped' into existence without a cause? As Craig puts it, 'it would take more faith for me to believe [in the universe's popping into existence uncaused out of nothing] than to believe that God exists'.[9] He holds that the second alternative is not a serious option for a reasonable person, and would only be entertained by a critic of the argument to try to block the move to the next step: given that the universe has a beginning, and that the beginning has a cause, what is this cause? Can we go any further in the argument and reason to any conclusions about the cause?

Supporters of this version of the argument, including Bonaventure and Craig, argue that we can go further. And as we will see, there is a lot of overlap at this stage in the reasoning with the other main version of the argument, which we shall consider in a moment. The cosmological argument points to a number of features of the cause of the universe. First, the cause must be *outside* the physical order, must be *non-physical* in some very important sense. This is because if we say that the cause is a physical cause, we can always ask what caused this (earlier, prior) physical cause? We know from general reasoning and from empirical science that every physical event has a prior cause, or to put the matter the other way around: no physical event in the universe is the cause of itself (or, to use the language of Thomas, every physical event is a contingent being). This is a crucial principle of the cosmological argument as a whole, and anyone who is inclined to doubt it is always free to submit an example of a physical event that caused itself! There can only be *one* first event, and it is this event which we are trying to explain, so the cause of it will logically have to be outside the physical order.

Second, the cause must be very powerful indeed in order to be capable of creating a universe like ours. Whether this means that the cause is all-powerful or not is an issue we will come back to in more detail in the chapter on the nature of God. Third, the cause is more likely to be an intelligent agent of some kind. This is a more reasonable alternative than saying that the cause is an impersonal force, or a non-physical, non-intelligent entity. Intelligence is also suggested by the order, beauty and meaning evident in the universe (we will elaborate this approach to the God question later in our discussion of the argument from design). But the creation of both the universe and of life, including human life, would seem to require by any reasonable standard a phenomenal intelligence. Fourth, the fact that the cause of the universe is an intelligent, rational being also suggests that the cause is a moral agent and a free being (this point relies in part on the moral argument for the existence of God, of which more in the next chapter). Fifth, the cause must also be a necessary being, a being who does not need a cause. This conclusion is justified by the fact that we are seeking an ultimate, not a local, cause. We will come back to this crucial point momentarily when we look at a second version of the cosmological argument. And so the cause of the universe is, to quote Thomas again, what all people normally call God.

ST THOMAS'S VERSION OF THE COSMOLOGICAL ARGUMENT

St Thomas Aquinas is famous for many things in philosophy and theology, but perhaps no more so than for his five arguments for the existence of God.[10] What is remarkable about these 'five ways' (*Quinque Viae*) is that they are so short! Of course, they have generated libraries-full of discussion. Thomas's arguments have been considerably modernized and elaborated in recent decades, in order particularly to take account of recent developments in science, and to respond to modern objections. The arguments appeal to the notions of motion and change, causation, degrees of perfection in nature and teleology, all familiar concepts to philosophers in the Middle Ages (and still familiar to us today). The basic idea behind all the arguments is that the universe needs an ultimate cause. However, Thomas's approach differs from the kalām approach, which we noted was originally based on the work of Thomas's contemporary and occasional sparring partner Bonaventure. Thomas disagreed with Bonaventure on the issue of whether the universe must have had a beginning. He was not convinced that logically the universe could not have had an eternal past. But what is interesting about his version of the argument is that he holds that even if the universe had an eternal past, it would *still* need an ultimate cause. This is why some believe that Thomas's version of the cosmological argument is more profound than Bonaventure's. I would argue that perhaps the strongest form of the cosmological argument is one that combines both forms, arguing initially that the universe must have a beginning (and so acknowledging the recent evidence from science), but then going on to show that even if it does not have a beginning, it still needs an ultimate cause.

The main thrust behind several of Thomas's arguments involves the intriguing notions of contingent and necessary being. A contingent being is a being which is not the cause of itself. In order for it to exist, it must have had some prior cause, otherwise it would not exist. And a contingent being also cannot last forever; at some point it will pass out of existence. A series of contingent beings linked together by cause and effect is called a contingent series. The universe, Thomas holds, is such a series. His question, therefore, is this: does the *number* of events in a contingent series help us with the question of the ultimate cause of the series? If the series has a finite number of events in it, the answer to our question is obviously no, since we would have a (contingent) first event in the series, an event which would not contain within itself the explanation of its own existence, as noted above. As Thomas put it in the Second Way: 'In the world of sensible things we find there is an order of efficient causes. There is no case known (neither is it, indeed, possible) in which a thing is found to be the efficient cause of itself, for so it would be prior to itself, which is impossible'.[11] But suppose that the contingent series of events is infinite – an actual infinite in the real world, such as the kind Craig has been arguing against? Does this help us with our initial question regarding the ultimate cause of the series? Thomas argues that it does not. This is because a contingent series of events still requires an ultimate explanation for its existence, *no matter how many members are in the series*. We can explain the local cause of any particular event, or sequence of events, by point- ing to prior causes in the series, but this will not, Thomas argues, help us to explain the existence of the *whole* series. We logically cannot find the cause of the whole contingent series within the series of events even if it is an infinite series. In this way, Thomas would say that those who think that if they can show the universe is an infi- nite series of physical events, as a way of *avoiding* asking what the ultimate or overall cause of the whole series is, are mistaken. It is still perfectly reasonable to ask how the whole series, with its infinite number of members, got here. And for this, Thomas argues, we must go *outside* the series.

Fr Frederick Copleston, a modern disciple of Thomas, has char- acterized the latter's version of the cosmological argument as one that appeals to the notion of a vertical series of causes (a 'hierarchy' of causes) of a particular event, rather than to the notion of a hor- izontal series of causes stretching back into the past.[12] The notion of a hierarchy of causes is evoked, Copleston believes, when one asks of a given event how it got here *as a whole, or overall*. He gives the example of a son who is dependent on his father, and the father is also dependent on his father, and so on. But there is another sense of dependent in which the son is not dependent on his father for the son's *present* activities. It is the former sense of 'dependent' that the cosmological argument is trying to convey. Any event in a series of events is never, according to this notion of 'dependent', the cause of itself. In addition, the whole series, because it is made up of contin- gent beings, can't be the cause of itself, so it *requires* a cause that is outside the series to explain its existence. A horizontal series, on the other hand, suggests the idea of causation, which is appealed to when we ask the cause of any given event in history. And the answer would be the preceding event, or events.

Looking at the cosmological argument from this point of view, Copleston develops Thomas's reasoning to point out that the fundamental idea behind the argument is not to probe the nature and cause of the series understood as a horizontal series, but to ask, hierarchically as it were, how the whole thing got here, no matter what its structure or size is. This point can also be expressed with reference to the concept of time. From Thomas's point of view, we are not looking particularly for what would be a preceding cause in time for any member of a temporal series of events, a series that had a beginning, or even that had no beginning. We are looking, rather, for an *atemporal* cause, a cause outside the realm of the series of events, an ultimate cause that is outside the temporal order of the whole series. This way of expressing the cosmological argument's main point emphasizes that the concepts of time, and of events and their prior causes in time, is not what is significant. What is significant is that any contingent series is in a crucial sense dependent, that there is a temporal order with events and causes in the first place. And this temporal order needs an ultimate cause, and this cause cannot itself be part of the temporal order.

This brings us to what many regard as the most powerful insight of the cosmological argument. This insight involves once again appeal to the concepts of necessary and contingent being. The significance of these concepts is sometimes overlooked or downplayed in contemporary expositions of the argument. But the essence of the cosmological argument is found in the conclusion that it is reasonable to say that *a necessary being exists*. This is because there are only two possible answers to the question of how the universe got here. The first is that it was created by a necessary being, a being who always existed, a being who cannot fail to be. Any other answer involving contingent beings would *not* provide us with an explanation of the universe, because we can always ask what caused this (contingent) being, and so on. Of course, Thomas knows that it is reasonable to wonder how a necessary being could exist, but the main point of his argument, I believe, is to illustrate that a necessary being *must* exist. That even if the concept looks odd at first, it is the most reasonable answer to our question about the ultimate origin of the universe; otherwise we would have no means of explaining its existence. When we reflect on the issue of the cause of the universe, we will see that we inevitably run into the probability of a necessary being. The only other answer one can give is to say that the universe has no ultimate cause, has no explanation, that it is just here. And the human mind strongly resists this answer, because it is so difficult to accept on a number of levels, the main one being that it is not logical. For Thomas, we know that the universe *must* have an ultimate cause, and we simply have to think about what the cause is like. And the only logical answer is that there must be a necessary being.

Some might reply to Thomas's reasoning by saying that the concept of a necessary being is unintelligible. What does it mean to say that there is a necessary being? How can there be a being who always existed, or who is the cause of itself? Surely this concept doesn't make any sense? Yet Thomas's point is that the cosmological argument is an argument that shows that the concept is quite intelligible, because such a being most probably exists. To look at this the other way around, when we begin to see that the only way to answer the question 'why is there something rather than nothing?' is to say that there must be a necessary being, this by itself gives intelligibility to the concept. And unless we have some other, independent, reason for rejecting the concept, we must accept that it is an intelligible concept.

Supporters of this version of the cosmological argument will agree that the question 'where did God come from?' is a perfectly legitimate one. It is not asked only by children, but one that the philosopher must think about as well. And Thomas argues that the answer that God is a necessary being is the best answer available. There are at least three other possible answers to this question. The first is that God was created by another God (or cause). But this is not satisfactory, because it does not give us an answer to the ultimate question. It still leaves us with the question of who caused this God; it indicates that God is just another contingent being whose existence requires a prior cause. The second is to say that there exists a group or committee of necessary beings. This is ruled out by Ockham's razor, the logical principle that, given two explanations for the same phenomenon, one should always choose the simplest one possible, all other things being equal – and one necessary being is all one needs to account for the existence of the universe. (This is also an argument for monotheism.) And the third answer is the one we started off with: to say that the concept of a necessary being is unintelligible. So unintelligible that when we come up against this notion at the end of the cosmological argument, it is unintelligible enough, or problematic enough, that the whole argument for the existence of God is scuttled. Dallas Willard has argued that we should reject the view that the concept of necessary being is unintelligible, because this is motivated by the question-begging move of assuming that physical existence is the only kind of existence one can have.[13] But the cosmological argument is an argument that shows that physical existence is very likely *not* the only kind of existence one can have; indeed, it is an argument about this very question. And so one cannot come to a conclusion on this question if the existence of God is yet to be decided. And Willard holds that the cosmological argument points clearly in the direction of a necessary being. Before moving on from these objections, it is important to note that traditional philosophers sometimes speak of God as self-caused, but this should not be taken to mean that God brings himself into existence, which would leave us with another problem. As Richard Taylor has noted: 'To say that something is self-caused (*causa sui*) means only that it exists, not contingently or in dependence upon something else, but by its own nature, which is only to say that it is a being which is such that it can neither come into being or perish.'[14] And, as Taylor observes, the cosmological argument is an argument intended to show that such a being very likely exists.

There are other objections to the argument besides the ones already mentioned. One other way of developing a criticism of the argument involves the denial of the principle of sufficient reason. The principle of sufficient reason was first formulated by Leibniz (1646–1716). It says that for every fact or event in the universe there is a reason for its existence. It would follow from this principle, therefore, as Leibniz argued, that there is a cause for the universe. This would be true whether the universe has an eternal past or whether it has a first event, say the Big Bang. Indeed, the principle of sufficient reason is one of the underlying principles of not just cosmological reasoning, but of human reasoning in general, as Leibniz points out. Yet some philosophers like Bertrand Russell and, more recently, William Rowe have responded to the cosmological argument by questioning the principle of sufficient reason. Russell questions it by suggesting that the universe is a 'brute fact'.[15] A brute fact is supposed to be a fact that does not need an explanation; it is just there. Yet, on its face, this is not a very convincing objection. It seems to be an ad hoc move concocted by some atheistic philosophers purely to block the cosmological argument. The concept of a brute fact is quite vague. It could mean that the universe does not need an explanation, or it might mean that although it needs an explanation, there is none available. If it means the former, then it seems false on any reasonable account of the nature of the universe. If it means the latter, then it seems to stop the debate about the existence of God too early, and implicitly suggests that physical existence is by definition the only kind of existence. It seems that one would need a better reason than this to slow down the argument.

Rowe, however, believes he has that reason.[16] He makes a deeper point about the principle of sufficient reason. He suggests that the desire to find an ultimate cause is based on the universal human desire to find a reason for everything in the universe. This is motivated by the natural curiosity of human beings, who want to know how things work and how they got here. And while he admits that this is a natural desire, it does not follow from the fact that we have this curiosity that there actually is a reason for everything. The principle of sufficient reason is a presupposition of reason almost, but as Rowe reminds us, William James said that nature is not bound to satisfy our presuppositions. Yet supporters of the argument have not found the questioning and even the denial of the principle of sufficient reason very convincing. This is because belief in the principle seems to be very reasonable even if we can't quite prove that it is an objectively true principle. In addition, the principle is supported by empirical science, in that we have never come across a physical event that does not require a cause; indeed, the idea that there might be a physical event that does not need a cause is almost unintelligible. It is one thing to say that we don't *know* the cause of a particular physical event, but it is far more radical to say that there is *no cause* for a particular event. Is it not more reasonable to accept the principle of sufficient reason and to seek the cause rather than to give up the argument too early? Many would agree that it is, but Rowe might say that, in normal cases, yes, it is reasonable to seek the cause, but the question of the cause of the universe is so perplexing that it might lead us legitimately to question the principle of sufficient reason. It seems, though, that if we accept the principle of sufficient reason in ordinary life, as well as in science, we should also accept it when thinking about the ultimate cause of the universe.

Other objections to the cosmological argument involve the claim that, although it might perhaps point to an overall cause of the universe, it does not give us the God of theism. It does not tell us very much about the nature of God. How does it show us, for example, that God is all loving, all good and all knowing, and so on? These are important questions. What can we know about the nature of God from the various arguments for God's existence? We will take up these questions more fully in our discussion of the nature of God in Chapter 4, though we have already noted that the cosmological argument gives us some reason to believe that the ultimate cause of the universe is powerful, non-physical, eternal and intelligent.

THE TELEOLOGICAL ARGUMENT

The teleological argument, or the argument from design, is one of the best-known arguments for the existence of God. It goes all the way back to the ancient Greeks, who were impressed with the apparent orderliness and purpose of the universe. Like the notion of the ultimate cause, the idea that the universe may show evidence of design cannot fail occasionally to cross the mind of anyone who reflects seriously on its nature and origin. When we contemplate the structure of the universe, even in a fairly cursory way, the question of whether it is the product of an intelligent mind is one that we naturally consider. I think most people would acknowledge that the universe shows on the surface at least some evidence of design or order in it, and that this is why the question of whether it is designed or not is a natural one for us to ask. But it does not necessarily follow from this that, when we examine the matter more deeply, design or order are really present. This leads us to take a more careful look at what we mean by 'design', what design in the universe might look like, and in what ways it might point to a designer.

The basic reasoning behind the argument from design is very straightforward. Although there are different versions of the design argument, they all have the same basic approach. The premise of the argument is that the universe shows evidence of design or order. This order can be seen through ordinary observation. The conclusion of the argument is that, since there is evidence of design, this means that there is probably an intelligent designer of the universe. The argument is an inductive or probabilistic one; it does not say that the design in the universe offers conclusive proof of a designer, but only that it is a very reasonable conclusion. Most proponents of the argument go further and say that it is the most reasonable conclusion.

The design argument is also an argument from analogy. The analogy is based on a comparison of the universe and its design with human artefacts which we have designed. The analogy is as follows: given that we can see design in many artefacts in the world, and we know that intelligent (human) minds are responsible for this (a car engine, a table, a furnished room), if we then find design in the universe, we can similarly infer that an intelligent mind is behind this design. Like most analogies, this one does not claim to be perfect in every respect. But it is strong, according to supporters of the argument, and enables us to conclude that the cause of the universe is most likely God, the intelligent designer.

Many would agree that the design argument is not only interesting, but intriguing. It raises all sorts of exciting questions that must be probed further if we are to flesh out the argument in a way that does it justice, and that helps us to appreciate the concepts and logical moves involved. The first concept we must examine further is the notion of design itself. In particular, what do we mean when we say that the universe *looks designed*? I noted above that it seems obvious that when we look around the universe, we would naturally think of it as being designed, at least some of the time. For example, we would see the planets in their orbits, we would observe a certain consistency in nature, we would see the order of the seasons, we would note that the universe can sustain life, that nature appears intelligible to the human mind, and so on. But while all these empirical observations suggest the idea of design, we need to think more deeply about whether they really are examples of design. Do they represent, or can they be elaborated as representing, design in the universe, in the same way that examining the parts of a car engine will reveal design, a design that clearly supports the conclusion that there is an intelligence behind a car engine? Supporters of the teleological argument believe that the design of the universe is indeed analogous to that of a car engine.

One way to define design is in the sense of 'purpose'. This was the way eighteenth-century philosopher William Paley understood the notion. Paley was a well-known champion of the idea of teleology in nature, a notion that goes back to the ancient Greeks, and especially the work of Aristotle, who argued that, from empirical observation, we can discover that nature has in-built purposes. As an illustration,

Paley uses the famous example of finding a watch in the wilderness. Supposing that we had never seen a watch before, Paley argues that we would conclude, after examining it carefully, that it was designed by a mind. It is too intricate an object to have come about by chance, which is the only other alternative, and it clearly seems to have been put together for a purpose (to tell time). But, Paley continues, if this is a reasonable way to argue about a watch, it is also a reasonable way to look upon nature itself. There are very intricate, complex, ordered operations in nature, and they could easily be said to have a purpose. Paley was particularly impressed by the physiological aspects of animals, and offered the example of the complex ordered operation of the human eye as evidence of clear design in nature. Animal habitats, he held, also seem perfectly designed for the animals that live in them. In addition, these animals seem to have a purpose in nature, as Aristotle argued, from which they never deviate. This argument can also be extended to human beings. We don't see our lives in terms of chance, but understand them in terms of purpose (not necessarily understood in a religious way: it wasn't for Aristotle). All of this, Paley concludes, suggests that there is a designer behind nature, that there must be a mind who thought up various purposes that would be part of nature, and put them into practice, as it were, just as the watchmaker did with the watch.[17] Building upon Paley's examples, Dallas Willard has suggested that if 'we stepped on an apparently uninhabited planet and discovered what, to all appearance, was a branch of the May Company or Sears – or even a Coke bottle or a McDonald's hamburger wrapper – it would be both psychologically impossible as well as flatly irrational in the light of our available data to believe that they came into existence without a design and a mind 'containing' that design. The extension of this conclusion to cover eyes, DNA structures and solar systems, by appropriate modification of premises, is only slightly less coercive.'[18]

This is one way to understand design in nature and, for a long time, it was the standard way of thinking about the design argument. But in recent times modern philosophers, most notably Richard Swinburne, have stressed another kind of design in the universe. This modern version is sometimes called the 'laws of science' or the 'laws of physics' argument. This argument says that if we examine the universe closely, especially through science, we discover that there are what are known as certain 'regularities' that occur in nature, empirically detectable patterns in how nature behaves. These have been codified and established as the laws of science, including most particularly the laws of physics and chemistry, perhaps the two most basic sciences (along with mathematics) for understanding the physical universe. We should also mention the laws of biology here, though some naturalists today attempt to reduce these, or to explain them, in terms of the laws of physics and chemistry. Examples of the laws of physics would include Newton's laws of motion (his third law states that for every action there is an equal and opposite reaction); Kepler's laws of planetary motion (his first law states that the planets circle around the sun in elliptical orbits, with the sun at one focus of the ellipse); Ohm's law relating to electrical circuits (which states that the relationship between voltage $\{V\}$, current $\{I\}$, and resistance $\{R\}$ is $V = I \times R$); and many others, both simple and complex. An example of a simple law from the point of view of the ordinary person might be that an object with a greater mass will crush an object with a lighter mass if it lands on top of it, all other things being equal. Or that an object with a lighter colour will be harder to see against a lighter background than a darker object. Or that rain will weaken the composition of wood, all other things being equal, and so on. These are ordinary everyday facts that we are familiar with in our experience, and, even though most of us may not often think of them as 'laws of science', their existence is remarkable from a philosophical point of view, and from the vantage point of asking ultimate questions about the universe.

The laws of physics argument holds that it is a quite remarkable fact that our universe follows laws consistently, with no exceptions. That nature obeys, and the behaviour of the objects of nature can be explained in terms of, the laws of physics is worthy of our attention. It seems reasonable to think that this underlying order in the universe was caused by an intelligent mind. This argument relies on the fact that if our universe really is a chance occurrence, and is innocent of any design, how is it that we live in a (scientifically) lawful universe rather than a lawless or chaotic one? It would be an amazing coincidence if the universe just so happened to be structured in this lawful way. The laws of physics make space travel possible, make electricity possible, made medicine possible, make mathematics possible, make science possible, make even the existence of life itself possible. In addition, these laws help us to understand how things work, and to improve our situation in the universe over time. It could have been the case that when we examined the world we found that there were no laws. German physicist Georg Ohm, for instance, might have found no consistent relationship between voltage, current and resistance, and so electrical theory as we know it would have been impossible. Or scientists working on electricity might have found that everything in the world was a conductor of electricity, making it too dangerous for everyday use. (This is an example of 'surface design' that intrigues people.) Or Kepler might have discovered that the planets did not move in any consistent way that could be pinned down, sometimes moving in a elliptical orbits, later in circular orbits, still later following no consistent path, and so no predictions about them being possible. One could object that if this was the case, human life would never have evolved either, and so we would not be here to worry about any of this. This is almost certainly true, but it does not alter the fact that this is the kind of universe that would very likely have existed – a scientifically lawless one – if the universe really were a product of chance. There is, therefore, an ultimate order to nature, which, as Swinburne explains, suggests a designer:

> If there is an explanation of the world's order it cannot be a scientific one, and this follows from the nature of scientific explanation . . . we explain the operation of scientific laws in terms of more general scientific laws . . . we explain the operation of Kepler's laws in terms of the operation of Newton's laws, and we explain the operation of Newton's laws in terms of the operation of Einstein's field equations for space relatively empty of matter. Science thus explains particular phenomena and low-level laws in terms of partly high-level laws. But from the very nature of science it cannot explain the highest-level laws of all; for they are that by which it explains all other phenomena.[19]

Philosophers have objected to the design argument in a number of ways. A few have challenged the notion of design on the basis that there really is no order present in the universe at all. The order we think we detect in nature is only apparent, not real. It is projected onto nature by the human mind, perhaps like seeing a face in the clouds when it is not really there. This argument is not taken very seriously by many supporters of the argument from design, because it is hard to see how the human mind projects, say, the laws of physics onto nature. This reply would further commit its proponents to epistemological relativism if they were seriously to advance it. That is to say, it would commit them to saying that all knowledge claims made about the physical world are projected onto it, and are not really about the world itself. But this would be to undermine science itself (and every other discipline), a high price to pay in order to press this particular critique of the design argument. (As we will see in later chapters, this will not be the only time that the cost of critiquing the data that form the basis of various theistic arguments comes with a high price, a point which illustrates the great *philosophical* significance of the debate over the existence of God.) It is surely much more reasonable to believe that the laws of nature are present in nature, and that we discover them, not invent them. This admission, though, requires us to face head on the question of how best to explain their existence. This first reply seems aimed more at dodging the design question than answering it.

The second line of objection is much more interesting. Proponents of this objection begin by acknowledging that there is order in the universe, but go on to argue that it most likely has a naturalistic, scientific explanation; the move to a supernatural explanation is therefore redundant. Some offer the theory of evolution as a good candidate for the natural explanation. Although I will discuss the theory of evolution more fully in the chapter on religion and science, let me take a moment here to sketch out how the theory is supposed to function as a natural explanation for the order in the universe. The theory of evolution is frequently offered as a reply to those like Paley who believe that there is purpose in nature, that nature is teleological, a view that, as noted, goes back to Aristotle. This objection to the design argument is based on a number of claims. The first is that the evolutionary process is a good explanation of the origin of life and of the origin of species. A second claim is that evolution occurs *randomly*, and involves significant chance occurrences along the way (in other words, evolution is not part of God's design plan, is not directed). Taken together, these claims mean that all of the species evolved *naturally* and by *chance* in the way that Charles Darwin described in his book *On the Origin of Species* (1859). But if all of the species originated by chance according to the process known as natural selection, this means that no species had to exist, no species is necessary, no species had to have the nature that it actually has. It also means, most importantly, that the thing that fascinated Paley so much – that species seem so perfectly designed for their particular habitats – now has a *natural* cause. The 'design' is only apparent, and is due to the process of natural selection, survival of the fittest, etc. While it looks like the habitat of the greenfly, for example, was perfectly designed for the greenfly to live in (if the greenfly was not green, it would not survive), it is not in fact designed at all, but naturally evolved like this over time. Not all species survived the process of natural selection, of course, but those that did, according to the theory of evolution, did so precisely because they were naturally suited, due to chance, to live in the particular environment they ending up living in. (A fuller account of the theory of evolution is presented in Chapter 7.)

This is an interesting reply to one version of teleology, that version which emphasizes the suitability of habitats for their species, the fact that nature seems to have been designed for a purpose. Evolution would seem to be an effective reply to any argument of the type offered by Paley, because, assuming that the theory is true, it would indeed give us a natural explanation for the purpose in nature that Paley concentrated on. Yet the theory of evolution applies only to biological systems. It really can't help us with the *origin* of matter and energy, and this is a mistake that some well-known contemporary scientists, such as Francis Crick and Richard Dawkins often make. They often talk as if evolution not only explains the origin and nature of species, but as if it can explain the origin of *everything*, including the universe. A moment's reflection will show that this is not the case. Evolution cannot help us with perhaps our two biggest questions on the subject of God's possible existence: i) how the universe came to be, what is its ultimate cause; and ii) how the design of the universe came about, 'design' here understood as the laws of physics. Well-known scientists, in particular, sometimes let their enthusiasm for the theory of evolution, which they want to see as a theory that can explain everything, dominate their supposed commitment to dispassionate reason and evidence Richard Dawkins' book *The Blind Watchmaker* is a good illustration of this phenomenon, and is an example of a famous scientist making a logical mistake. Dawkins, and others, overlook the point that evolution is not a theory about the origin of matter and energy. In order for evolution to occur, it is necessary to have already existing matter present in some kind of environment. And so evolution *logically cannot* be an account of the origin of the universe. The theory of evolution is not enough to solve the main problem facing a naturalistic account of origins: where did the first matter and energy come from?

Coming back more directly to the argument from design, which we are discussing here, evolution also cannot give us an explanation for the laws of physics. This is because evolution, like all scientific theories, must *presuppose* these laws. Evolution is a theory of change, explaining how species evolve over time in particular environments. But the key point is that these changes will happen in accordance with the laws of physics. The matter and energy involved will behave, or follow, or obey the laws of physics in ways we have discovered in science. So, for example, when a predator kills a slow cheetah (so that all we are left with eventually are fast cheetahs), this is because of the scientific laws that, all other things being equal, objects moving at fast speeds can overtake objects moving at slower speeds, and objects with large mass can kill objects with less mass. Or when the water poisons a particular species of fish, this is because of the law that the particular chemical in the water destroys the cell structure, say, of this particular species of fish. These are all basic laws of nature that we progressively discover, codify and elaborate by means of the various sciences. Evolution is not an explanation of them; rather it operates according to them. It is these laws that the second version of the design argument is based on. As Charles Taliaferro has noted, 'Reigning accounts of biological evolution (and their successors) do not address questions about why there are any such evolutionary laws at all, or any organisms to begin with.'[20]

The philosopher David Hume was well known for advancing several interesting criticisms of the design argument, which adopt a third strategy. Many of Hume's criticisms were aimed at making the general point that, while there might be order in the universe, the argument from analogy is not a very good one. It is generally a mistake, Hume argued, to reason from the fact that ordered things are made by (our) intelligent minds to the conclusion that the world is ordered, and so there must be a Supreme Mind behind it. Hume attacked the argument from analogy at several points, and for a long time his criticisms were taken very seriously by philosophers on all sides of the debate. This is less true today, as supporters of the design argument believe that Hume's objections have little effect on modern versions of the argument. Supporters of the design argument tend to hold that the analogy, while not perfect, is based on reasonable similarities concerning design and designers, while critics of the argument tend to stress the dissimilarities. The reader should consider Hume's objections with this point in mind, as you try to make a judgement as to which side has the better argument.

At least one of Hume's objections can be dismissed quickly. The argument from design, he contended, does not show us that God is omnipotent, omniscient and so on. He appeals to a principle to make this point: 'when we infer any particular cause from an effect, we must proportion the one to the other, and can never be allowed to ascribe to the cause any qualities but what are exactly sufficient to produce the effect.' Richard Swinburne is one contemporary philosopher who has responded in detail to Hume's criticisms of the argument.[21] Swinburne agrees with Hume that the design argument does not by itself give us the traditional view of God. But the primary aim of the argument, Swinburne continues, is to show that there *is* a designer, and what can be gleaned about the nature of the designer is a secondary question. It is not that nothing can be determined about the nature of God from the argument, but we would need further arguments to get the traditional attributes of God, for example. But Swinburne argues that the stated principle to which Hume appeals is too strict. If we accepted it, we would have to abandon science. This is because it is always possible to infer rationally from the cause of an event, E, more than just that it can produce E. If this were all we could conclude, we would be unable to add anything to our knowledge when we reasoned to the cause of an event, and this would be manifestly to compromise the whole scientific enterprise.

Hume formulates two objections based on the uniqueness of the world, and the difficulty in concluding that it is analogous to human artefacts. I call this the 'one-world' objection. The argument, as I have noted, has two emphases. The first is that the analogy fails because there is only one world. If we had several worlds that we knew were caused by gods, then, by analogy, we could reason to the probable cause of any new world under discussion as being a god. Just as if we bought several pairs of shoes at a certain store, and they had always been of good quality, we can infer that, analogously, another pair from the same store will be of good quality. But if we are dealing with a different, unique object – a new bicycle say – bought from the same store, our argument would be weaker if our analogous reasoning was based on our experience with shoes. One can see from a moment's reflection that Hume's objection is not clear-cut. The strength or weakness of the argument depends in part on what we are buying and on the type of store. One could perhaps conclude that if the object we bought from the store was radically different from the type of objects we usually buy there, that the analogous reasoning might be weak. But this might not always be a reasonable conclusion, because the store might have an excellent reputation for quality goods overall. In other words, we must look very carefully at how objects are being compared to see if the similarities outweigh the differences. And so it is with the universe. Perhaps Hume is showing in this objection the inadequacy of the scientific method of his day. Current science shows us that, as Swinburne puts it, if we observe that A*s are similar to As in some important and relevant respect, and As were caused by a mind, then A*s were probably caused by a mind. And A* and A are similar because they both show evidence of order or design.

The second emphasis in Hume's argument seems to be that we cannot use an argument from analogy if one of the items in the argument is the only one of its kind. But is this true? On its face, it would seem to be a false principle since we are reasoning all the time about the universe, and indeed the human race, even though they are the only instances of their kind. Some might wonder if these are good examples since many of our conclusions about the universe and the human race are not always based on analogous forms of reasoning. Yet some of our conclusions are based on analogous reasoning, and such reasoning is dominant in many areas of life, not just in science. In addition, the fact that the universe is the only one of its kind might not be of much importance for the form of analogy employed in the design argument, because the key feature of the argument is design, and we have other instances of design in nature, namely those we have produced, so we are mainly considering similarities here after all, not differences or uniqueness.

Hume offers two other objections which revolve around the move to the existence of a designer. The first is that if we are going to say there is a designer based on the evidence of design in nature, shouldn't we be able to explain the designer? This is an interesting objection, and obviously the nature of the designer is important. But it is no real criticism of the argument from design to say that it doesn't explain the nature of the designer. The main aim of the argument is to show firstly that there *is* a designer, and then later we may be able to say something further about the nature of the designer, both positive (the designer has power and knows mathematics and logic) and negative (the designer is not like man). This last point is important, because sometimes this objection is pressed by Hume and his followers to say that we should conclude that the designer is like man, if we are going to use the analogy of the human mind creating things. But again the point is that analogies are not perfect. No analogy says that objects are alike in every respect, and there are obvious differences between the world and human artefacts (a statue, a house, an engine) to enable us to conclude that the power and intelligence of the designer is on a vastly different scale to ours. We can't make a world, but the designer of the universe can, and so there is justification for concluding that the cause of the universe cannot be a human being. What about saying then that, like with a house or an engine, the cause of the universe is a group of human beings? Would this not be a closer analogy if we are going to base our analogy on human intelligence and power? Why only one God? Supporters of the argument have replied to this point by appeal to the principle of Ockham's razor (mentioned above). This principle says that, if two hypotheses explain something equally well, then, all other things being equal, it is more logical to opt for the simplest explanation of the two. 'Simplest' here does not mean easier to understand, but refers to the explanation that has the least amount of explanatory material in it to bring about the effect. And so, if we apply this principle, we can conclude that there is one designer of the universe, because one designer is all we need to do the job. It is not necessary to postulate more than one designer.

A different type of response to the argument from design brings us back to the theory of evolution again, and to what philosophers call the problem of evil. Some critics invoke the existence of evil in the world as an argument against design. The basic point behind the problem of evil objection is that the existence of evil in the world is evidence that there is no God, because evil seems to be a kind of disorder, disunity, or chaos, a blight on the natural order of things in the universe, and so its presence suggests that there is as much chaos in the world as there is design. This is one version of the problem of evil objection against the existence of God. It does not ask, as the main version does, why God allows evil, but rather argues that the presence of evil in the world points to the presence of disorder, and this is counter-evidence to the evidence of design. The claim is that the argument from design is weakened considerably if, in addition to the order in the universe, we see a lot of disorder as well. This might suggest that there is no mind behind things after all. The problem of evil objection is a serious one for theism, and one that deserves a chapter all to itself (Chapter 5). Let us just say, in reply to this particular form of the objection, that the presence of evil would not be counter-evidence to the order in the universe if the order is understood as the laws of physics. Indeed, the laws of physics at the practical, everyday level make the existence of evil, as well as good, possible. It is because of the consistency of the laws of physics that the bullet harms the person, that the airplane crashes, that the town floods. But this objection might be a more difficult problem for the notion of design understood in terms of purpose. This is especially true if we interpret the notion of purpose in a broad sense, to include the view that nature tends towards the good, that the aim of the universe is good, that God's creation is good, even that this is the best of all possible worlds (did God create the best world he could have, and if not, why not?). We will come back to these troubling objections and questions in the chapter on the problem of evil.

It is necessary at this point to mention briefly the objection that evolution itself is evidence *against* design in the universe. This topic will be addressed more fully in the chapter on religion and science, but it is helpful to introduce the problem here, a problem that some have claimed evolution creates for religious belief. Well-known evolutionary biologist Stephen J. Gould has argued, for instance, that if we examine the processes of evolution closely, they do not seem to show evidence of design.[22] Quite the contrary, Gould argues: the whole process seems to show evidence of randomness, chance occurrences, dead ends and lucky breaks. Evolution involves a lot of waste, many adaptations do not work, some species survive but in difficult circumstances, all evidence, it is claimed, against evolution having any order or design behind it. Now, of course, we have already pointed out how evolution is not an argument against the laws of physics version of the argument from design. But Gould and others have argued that it may be an argument *against* teleology in nature. And because it is an argument against teleology in nature, some have adopted the theory as a type of general argument for atheism. Richard Dawkins has claimed, for example, that he can't imagine how anyone could have been an atheist before 1859 (the year *On the Origin of Species* first appeared), and has famously asserted that 'Darwin made it possible to be an intellectually fulfilled atheist',[23] which is to say that, according to Dawkins, evolution is an argument against teleology, whether Darwin ever intended this, or ever used it in this way himself (his friends certainly did, including Thomas Huxley). The view that evolution is an argument against design is such a popular one in certain intellectual circles that any contemporary discussion of the argument today (and indeed of the general case for theism) has to give this theory serious attention. This is why every educated person, especially if one is seriously interested in the religion vs. secularism debate, should have an understanding of the main claims of the theory of evolution, and their philosophical, theological and moral implications. For evolution is an unusual scientific theory in that it has profound implications for these other areas, unlike most scientific theories. Although it is in the context of the argument from design that the theory of evolution often comes up, it has interesting implications for the overall debate between religious belief and secularism. This important topic deserves a full discussion in itself, and will be a major theme of Chapter 7.

THE ANTHROPIC ARGUMENT FROM DESIGN

It would not be appropriate to end our discussion of the design argument without providing a brief overview of a still newer version of the argument that has emerged in the last few decades, a fascinating version that has received significant attention. Known as the 'anthropic argument', or sometimes as the 'anthropic principle', this version revolves around the concept of what has been called the 'fine-tuning' of the universe. The basic idea is that current science, especially in cosmology, astronomy and astrophysics tells us that, given the nature of the processes involved in the Big Bang, the probability of the right conditions occurring on earth by chance for the support and sustaining of life is extremely low, so low as to be almost incalculable. Some thinkers have concluded that the probability of our universe being suitable to sustain life is as low as one in ten billion. Elaborating just a little further, the anthropic argument holds that there are several factors that had to have been just right in the Big Bang in order for the universe to be able to support life. These conditions are causally independent of each other, and the probability of each occurring is extremely low, let alone all of them occurring together. These conditions, according to Stephen Hawking, include:

i) the rate of expansion of the universe – Hawking holds that a reduction in the rate of expansion of the Big Bang of one part in a hundred thousand million million would have led to a recollapse of the universe, while a similar increase would also have produced a different universe than the one that we have; and ii) the nature of electrons – if the electrical charge of the electron had been only slightly different, stars would either have been unable to burn hydrogen and helium, or else they would not have exploded to create the heavy elements.[24] Similar arguments have been made relating to the degree of gravitational force and the strong and weak nuclear forces.

Proponents of the anthropic argument point out that these facts are just as remarkable as the fact that the universe has laws. And that when one reflects on what they mean, one is justified in concluding that they point to the conclusion that the universe was designed specifically to make life as we know it possible. This argument does not say that the existence of *a* universe was improbable, but that the existence of *our* universe was so improbable as to be not worth taking seriously. We only have two alternatives: that it was deliberately set up by an intelligent mind to support the existence of life, or that it is simply a remarkable coincidence that it should do so. The latter alternative is hard to believe given the staggering improbabilities involved. The universe, as astronomer Fred Hoyle is reported to have observed, looks like 'a put up job'! This argument is difficult to refute. The Big Bang theory clearly supports the evidence appealed to in the arguments, and the probabilities involved. Although there is undoubtedly some speculation involved in any actual calculation of the probabilities, there seems little doubt that the general point is valid – that the probabilities involved are incalculably low, even if we cannot be precise about the exact figures involved.

Some critics respond by appealing to the 'multiple universes' theory. The basic claim of this theory is that our universe is only one among many alternative universes. Looked at from this point of view, the probability of at least one of these universes being able to support life would, therefore, be higher. Here is Michael Martin on the design argument in general: 'The improbability of life may be the result of many gods or of impersonal creative forces. Moreover, cosmologists have developed an alternative naturalistic explanatory model in terms of so-called world ensembles. They have conjectured that what we call our universe – our galaxy and other galaxies – may be one among many alternative worlds or universes . . . given enough universes it is very likely that in some of these the complex conditions necessary for life would be found.'[25]

The reader should ponder these alternative explanations of design. Is the conjecture of 'world ensembles' too speculative, too ad hoc to serve as an effective rejoinder to the anthropic argument? Does it ignore the rational significance of undisputed scientific evidence contained in the Big Bang? Or is it a reasonable suggestion required by the ever more ambitious search for scientific explanations of unusual phenomena? Sometimes students will raise a different objection to this version of the design argument. They argue that since life on earth obviously exists, the universe had to have been the sort of universe that would produce us and so when we look back to the beginning, the conditions we encounter would obviously be suited to support life, because it is these ordered conditions that produced us! This is true, but it doesn't alter the fact that there might have been no order in the Big Bang such that would produce life. It could have been the case, for example, that when we discovered the ingredients that make up the Big Bang, we also discovered that almost any combination of ingredients would have likely supported the existence of life. Instead, we find that the ingredients necessary to produce life are extremely hard to come by – recall the low probabilities – and yet they emerged from the Big Bang. As J.C.C. Smart has noted, 'It is the fine tuning that (partially) explains the existence of observers, not the existence of observers that explains the fine tuning.'[26]

We need to think of ourselves for a moment as observing the universe and its activities from an external vantage point. From that vantage point, we would either see a universe that is chaotic, both at the beginning and in its course, and that cannot produce life, or one that has an order and regularity to it, that enables life to exist. We would also observe that the possibility of the universe (given the conditions present in the Big Bang) being able to support life is extremely improbable, and this would suggest that it might be 'a put up job'. It is logically possible that our universe could have happened by chance: this conclusion cannot be totally ruled out. Yet we must also reflect on whether or not it is a *probable* conclusion. Is it as likely as the proverbial monkey sitting in front of a typewriter hitting the keys at random and just happening to type out a perfect copy of *Moby-Dick*? And that remarkable improbability, and its implications for the concept of design, are the central insights of the anthropic argument.

CHAPTER 3

NECESSARY BEING, MORALITY AND MIRACLES

THE ONTOLOGICAL ARGUMENT

The ontological argument for the existence of God was first proposed in the eleventh century by St Anselm (1033–1109), Archbishop of Canterbury. Since then it has had many restatements, most notably in the work of René Descartes and G. W. Leibniz and, in more recent times, in the work of Norman Malcolm and Charles Hartshorne. In fact, there has been a considerable revival of interest in the argument in recent decades. It is the subject of continuing debate, and is always good for provoking a reaction from undergraduates in particular. Our aim here is to provide an overview of some of the main forms of the argument, and of the critical discussion the argument has provoked.

There has been some debate as to whether, with the ontological argument, Anselm was presenting a purely rational argument for the existence of God, or something less than that. Anselm had been strongly influenced by St Augustine, and like Augustine he believed that faith had a certain primacy over reason, and so he would not normally have seen it as a priority to demonstrate the existence of God. But Anselm is also well known for the view that reason can help us to understand what we believe in our faith. 'I do not seek to understand so that I may believe', he famously wrote, 'but I believe so that I may understand.'[1] He had discussed the cosmological argument in an earlier work, the *Monologion*, but in a later work, the *Proslogion*, he tells us that he began to wonder if a single argument could be found which would constitute an independent proof for the existence of God and which would suffice by itself to demonstrate that (1) God truly (really) exists, that (2) He is the supreme Good . . . and that

(3) He is whatever else we believe about the divine substance.[2] Anselm believed he had found such an argument in the ontological argument. (The name 'ontological argument' was not coined by Anselm, but was first used by Kant in his *Critique of Pure Reason*).

The ontological argument differs from the arguments we looked at in the previous chapter in its basic approach to the question of God's existence. The first cause and design arguments are *a posteriori* arguments. This means that the premises of the arguments are known to be true, based on facts of experience; these arguments begin with certain facts of our experience and reason to conclusions about God based on these facts. The ontological argument does not take the same approach. It is, rather, an *a priori* argument. An *a priori* argument is one where the premises and conclusions are known to be true *independently* of experience, one which is not based on any appeal to experience. So what Anselm is seeking is an argument that will show that there is a God by examining the concept, or idea, of God only. He believes that he has discovered a way to show that God exists, which is based solely on an examination of the *concept* of God. This approach goes against the usual way of arguing for God's existence, which is to look at any empirical evidence available in the universe, and then reason *a posteriori* to the existence of God. Anselm's approach has generated much attention, not only because his argument is intriguing, but because it is so bold. For how can it be possible to examine the concept or idea of something and then to reason to its existence based on our reflections about the concept alone? Anselm holds that, in the case of God, this is possible; that when we attend carefully to this special, indeed unique, concept we will come to see that God must exist.

Anselm begins the argument by noting that religious believers and unbelievers alike mean by 'God', 'something than which nothing greater can be conceived'.[3] And the essence of the ontological proof is that, given this understanding of God, one cannot deny God's existence without contradiction. It is generally agreed in modern scholarship that the argument can be best understood by distinguishing between two forms:

(1) A being is greater if it exists in reality that if it exists in the understanding. Therefore, God, who is the greatest being, must exist.

(2) A being is greater if it necessarily exists that if it continently exists. Therefore, God necessarily exists.

Anselm himself never clearly distinguished between these two forms of the argument, but it is claimed by some contemporary thinkers, most notably Norman Malcolm, that it is best to do so, because although certain criticisms may be true of the first form, they are not true of the second.

Let us begin by analysing the first form of the argument, which will enable us to provide an exposition of Anselm's general line of reasoning. Anselm is concerned to show that, given our understanding of God as 'something than which nothing greater can be conceived', the existence of God cannot be denied without contradiction. To illustrate this point further, he makes a distinction between an object existing in reality (*in re*), and existing in the understanding (*in intellectu*), and claims that if a being were to exist in the understanding only, then a greater being than this being can be conceived, namely a being who exists in reality. Now God, whom we conceive as the greatest possible being, as that 'than which none greater can be conceived', must exist in reality, for if God existed in the understanding only, then God would not be the most perfect being. That is to say, if we conceive of God as existing in the understanding only, then we have not conceived of God as the greatest possible being, because a being conceived of as existing would be a greater being. As Anselm puts it: 'And certainly that than which a greater cannot be conceived cannot stand only in relation to the understanding. For if it stands at least in relation to the understanding, it can be conceived to be also in reality, which is greater.'[4] So, according to Anselm, as well as having several attributes like omniscience, omnipotence, and so on, God also possesses the attribute (or property or characteristic) of *existence in reality*. This is part of what we mean by 'God'. Existence in reality seems to be regarded by Anselm as yet another perfection of God.

The first form of the argument has been criticized by Gaunilo in Anselm's own time, and by Kant later on, as well as by many modern writers, on the grounds that existence is *not* a perfection of things. Gaunilo, a contemporary of Anselm, raised the objection that perhaps most readily comes to mind when thinking about the ontological argument for the first time. The reasoning is unsound, Gaunilo says, because one could use it to demonstrate the existence of a perfect *anything*. For example, we could use the argument to prove the existence of a perfect island on exactly the same grounds from which Anselm had deduced the existence of God. The perfect island, defined as 'more excellent than all lands' must exist, Gaunilo held, for if it does not then 'any other land that exists in reality would be more excellent than this island, and this island, which you understand to be the most excellent of all lands, would then not be the most excellent'.[5] Gaunilo is saying that if one denies that the perfect island (which we agree to think of as the *most* perfect island) is not the most perfect island because an island which really existed would be greater, then we have simply *failed* to conceive properly of the perfect island. In particular, we have failed to conceive of it *as existing*. But, of course, the argument cannot be used to show the existence of a perfect island, and likewise, cannot be used to show that God exists.

Unfortunately, Gaunilo makes the mistake of conceiving the perfect island as being greater than all other existing things rather than all other conceivable ones. He has failed to attend fully to the concept of God. Anselm rejected his criticism on this point, because Anselm held that God's existence is *unique*. That 'than which none greater can be conceived' is a concept that can only be applied to God. This is not because he is singling God out for special attention, or trying to prove that God exists by definition, but because, logically, there can only be *one* greatest being, and this is God. So if we *conceive* of the greatest possible being, this being must exist, and will be God. The ontological argument cannot be used to prove the existence of anything else. It only works for one being – the greatest being – 'a greater than which cannot be conceived'. This description can logically apply only to one being, and that is God.

Yet, some believe that Gaunilo's criticism contains the seeds of a valid line of attack against the argument. Immanuel Kant has tried to state Gaunilo's criticism more trenchantly: 'By whatever and however many predicates we may think a thing – even if we completely determine it – we do not make the least addition to the thing when we further declare that the thing is. Otherwise, it would not be exactly the same thing that exists, but something more than we had thought in the concept and we could not, therefore, say that the exact object of my concept exists.'[6]

Kant is denying that the existence of an object can be a property (or a perfection) of the object. This is because it adds nothing to a thing, as Anselm claims it does. Its function, rather, is to posit or affirm a reality corresponding to a concept, and so Kant argues that Gaunilo's initial criticism is justified. For Gaunilo's point was that Anselm must show that this island's excellence (or perfection) is in my understanding only in the way that a thing which really exists is in my understanding and not in the way that a thing which is merely possible or doubtfully real is in my understanding. But this can only be done if we could show that the perfect island existed, and corresponded to our concept. But if existence can only be regarded as connoting a reality corresponding to our concept, then it would not be correct to say that a thing is greater if it exists in reality than if it exists in the understanding. It is only true to say that if it exists in reality, then it corresponds to our concept. But this would not be enough to show that existence in reality is a property of the concept of God, because this only means that nothing can be called God unless he really exists. This may be true, but it would not prove that God exists. Anselm has not taken the distinction between things and concepts seriously, and consequently (in this first form of the ontological argument) has not proved the existence of God, according to Kant. This brings us to the second form of the argument.

As noted above, some thinkers, including Norman Malcolm, have held that a second form of the ontological argument is distinguishable in the third chapter of the *Proslogion*, a form which states that even if contingent existence (referred to in the first form) is not a perfection of God, *necessary* existence is, and it follows from this that God necessarily exists by definition.[7] The distinction between contingent and necessary existence is one we have already had occasion to employ in our discussion of the cosmological argument in Chapter 1. We noted there that a contingent being is a being who did not have to exist, whose existence depends upon something else, a being who (or which) is not in metaphysical control of its own existence. On the other hand, a necessary being is a being who always existed, whose existence does not depend upon anything else. To put this point in terms of concepts, we might say that a necessary being is a being who cannot be conceived not to exist, whereas a contingent being is a being who can be conceived not to exist. And the second form of the argument makes the point that this is what Anselm means when he focuses on the concept of God. For Anselm, God is a being who cannot be conceived not to exist: he is a necessary being. And so, Anselm argues, that the fool of the Psalm (14.1) who says in his heart there is no God is talking about God's existence as if it were a contingent existence, as if God were a contingent being. But God's existence is necessary, God is the being who cannot fail to be. And it is impossible to hold that a necessary being might not exist. Necessary existence, according to this version of Anselm's argument, is involved in the very concept of God. The fool understands that God is supposed to be conceived of as a necessary being, yet he still thinks that God just happens to exist for eternity (so he really sees God as a *contingent* being, who just so happens always to exist). Yet, this form of the argument suggests that if we really attend to this unique concept we see that God necessarily exists, which means that he cannot fail to be.

Before turning to some problems philosophers have raised with this view, we should note that in recent discussions of the ontological argument some have advanced the argument that the notion of necessary being has two meanings, and that it is important for our understanding of the ontological argument that we keep them distinct. It is possible to distinguish between a logically necessary being and a factually necessary being. Malcolm argues that Anselm is referring to the concept of a logically necessary being; he asserts, moreover, that such an interpretation is immune from traditional criticism. A logically necessary being is a being whose existence cannot be denied without contradiction. A factually necessary being, on the other hand, is a being whose existence depends only on itself, not on any other being. It is far from clear, though, that this is a helpful distinction, and it does not seem to be faithful to Anselm's texts. It seems that factually necessary being is what Anselm means, and what we generally mean when we say that God is a necessary being. The concept of a logically necessary being seems to come too close to saying that God exists by definition. John Hick has argued that Anselm was referring to factually necessary being, and conceived God as 'sheer, ultimate, unconditioned reality, without origin or end', as a factually necessary being.[8] It is hard to agree, after a careful reading of the *Proslogion*, that Anselm was using a notion of 'necessary' different from the standard view. His own contemporaries, like Gaunilo, would surely have first picked up on this discrepancy. The necessity that Anselm refers to with regard to God lies in the fact that God has an independent and eternal existence, and is not dependent on anything outside himself.

However, even if Anselm did not refer to God as a logically necessary being, it is still an option which is, according to Malcolm and

Charles Hartshorne, applicable to the ontological argument; it is an option, therefore, which must be considered. Malcolm holds that when the concept of God is correctly understood as a concept of a logically necessary being, one sees that one cannot deny the existence of God without contradiction, because one is not doing justice to the concept of God. He writes: 'Once one has grasped Anselm's proof of the necessary existence of a being greater than which cannot be conceived, no question remains as to whether it exists or not.'[9] Charles Hartshorne has elaborated this point. Hartshorne holds that if the idea of God is not nonsensical, then God must exist.[10] This is because the existence of God cannot be merely 'possible'. Hartshorne agrees with Malcolm that a necessary being is either impossible or actual.[11] He goes on to argue that self-existence is a predicate which necessarily and uniquely belongs to God for it is part of the predicate 'divinity'. Hartshorne forcefully adds that the ontological argument is often construed as saying that if the necessary being happens to exist – that is, if as mere contingent fact it exists – then it exists not as contingent fact, but as necessary truth. This is, of course, ludicrous, but it is a misformulation of the argument, according to Hartshorne. What we should be saying is that 'if the phrase necessary being has a meaning, then what it means exists necessarily, and if it exists necessarily, then, a fortiori, it exists'. Another way of saying this, he holds, is to say that 'that which exists, if at all, necessarily' is the same as 'that which is conceivable, if at all, only if it exists'. And since it is conceivable, the necessary being is, therefore, actual. Hartshorne and Malcolm hold that it is not existence that is a property of God, but *necessary* existence.

Yet, on closer reflection, we might reasonably ask whether it is correct to say that logically necessary being is a perfection of God. If God is understood as a logically necessary being, it is hard to see how this does not mean that the statement 'God exists' is true by definition. But to say this would be to dodge the issue of a proof of the actual existence of God. Of course, there is a sense in which to say that God is a necessary being implies that God is a logically necessary being, but this is only true if God *actually* exists. (Thomas Aquinas makes this point, in his critique of the ontological argument, by saying that, unlike every other created thing, God's existence is in itself self-evident – God's existence *is* his essence – but Aquinas thinks that this fact is not self-evident *to us*.) Since a necessary being is a being who cannot fail to be, then, if there were such a being, there would be a sense in which God's existence would be logically necessary. But to establish this conclusion, we would surely have to know that God actually existed. To put the matter the other way around, *only if we know that God is a factually necessary being could we know that God's existence is also logically necessary*, and so factual necessity must have priority.

Malcolm's contention seems to be that, unless God is conceived as a logically necessary being, he cannot be regarded as an all-perfect God, because if we conceive God as a factually necessary being then his existence can be doubted. But it is impossible to doubt God's existence, according to Malcolm, because this would involve a contradiction in the very concept of God. If we can doubt God's existence, he seems to be saying, we have not fully attended to the concept of God. So God must be understood as a logically necessary being. But is Malcolm right about this? It seems quite possible to *conceive* of God as an all-perfect, yet factually necessary being, and also still to wonder whether or not this God exists. All one would be saying, in effect, is that God's existence can be doubted, because we have not established that God, conceived as a necessary being, actually exists. It seems that it is always legitimate to doubt the existence of God from a metaphysical point of view. It is true that a particular individual might not be able to bring herself to doubt God's existence from a psychological point of view, but we are talking about metaphysical doubt here.

This problem with the notion of a logically necessary being – that it is possible to deny the existence of God without contradiction – may be fatal to the whole ontological argument. For if it is possible to deny the existence of God without contradiction, then the claim that God is a necessary being (in the second form of the argument) does not, in fact, prove the existence of God, as Anselm, and later Hartshorne, claimed. The problem has again been well formulated by Kant: 'To posit a triangle, and yet to reject its three angles, is self-contradictory; but there is no contradiction in rejecting the triangle together with its three angles. The same holds true of the concept of an absolutely necessary being. If its existence is rejected, we reject the thing itself with all its predicates, and no question of contradiction can then arise.'[12]

Only if one knew that the concept 'that than which none greater can be conceived' was not self-contradictory – i.e., *if one knew that God actually existed* – could one accept the ontological argument as formulated by Anselm and his followers. But we do not know whether there is such a being, or whether there could be such a being. And it is precisely on our knowing this that the ontological argument seems to depend. This is what Thomas Aquinas means when he says that the concept of God is not self-evident to us. If it were self-evident, then the ontological argument would work, because we would see that God exists! But we cannot see this because we cannot be sure, from our limited vantage point as human beings, whether or not the concept of factually necessary being is contradictory. We may believe that it very probably is not contradictory (as we saw in our earlier discussion of the cosmological argument). But we are not certain, and it seems that we need certainty for an *a priori* argument for the existence of God to succeed. Noting that the existence of a necessary being is probable would not be enough to demonstrate that God exists from an analysis of the concept of God alone, though Alvin Plantinga and others are right to say that we cannot simply dismiss the ontological argument on the grounds that the concept of necessary being is incoherent, as they believe Hume and Kant come close to doing. But even if we take the concept seriously, and believe that it is very probably intelligible, the ontological argument seems to stretch the case too much by arguing that we can move to the actual existence of God from a study of the concept alone.

GOD AND MORALITY

Several philosophers have argued for a moral argument for the existence of God, among them Immanuel Kant, John Henry Newman and C.S. Lewis. The moral argument is another of those arguments (along with the first cause and design arguments) that appeals to the intuitions of the ordinary person. The basic idea behind the argument is that the existence of objective moral values, and the whole objective moral order, is best justified if God exists. The argument is concerned with the justification of our ordinary moral experience, and asks the question: how are objective moral values best justified? The argument is not asking if one can actually live a moral life if one does not believe in God, nor is it asking how God chooses the moral values that become the basis of the moral order. The argument is, rather, based on the insight that it is one thing to hold and practise objective moral values, but it is another, more difficult, project to justify these values. We know that Hitler's genocide against the Jews was morally wrong, and that Lincoln's freeing of the slaves was morally right; that the school yard bully who steals his neighbour's lunch money has done something wrong, and that the businessman who makes a large anonymous donation to his local charity has done something morally commendable. These value judgements appeal to an objective moral order. While we might not always agree on what is objectively moral (though Lewis argues that we sometimes underestimate the moral agreement across cultures), we have a bedrock belief that there *is* an objective order, and that some things are clearly right and some clearly wrong. Kant puts this by saying that there are two things that fill the mind with awe and admiration: 'the starry heavens above me and the moral law within me'. The conclusion of the moral argument is that the religious worldview offers a better, more plausible overall explanatory account of the justification of this objective moral order than the secularist worldview.

Like most arguments for the existence of God, the moral argument has several different versions. We will look first at the form of the argument made famous by Kant, and then at a more general version one might accept even if one were not a follower of Kant. Kant's argument is a consequence of his moral theory, which is a fascinating, complex and highly debated theory. Fortunately, we only need an overview of the basic themes of Kant's moral theory in order to appreciate his moral argument for the existence of God. Kant argues that the only thing that is good without qualification, that is intrinsically good or good in itself, is the good will. But a good will is a will that acts for the sake of duty, not desire. We do what is right, according to Kant, because we *ought* to do it, not because we like doing it necessarily, or because it is in our self-interest to do it. He goes on to argue that rational and free beings, like human beings, follow objective moral maxims; these are formal moral principles aimed at doing what is right for its own sake, and not because we are aiming at some overall good or end. By founding moral motivation on these kinds of maxims, Kant argues that we would perform the correct moral action more often than not, whereas if we base our moral motivation too closely on our desires (on what we *like* to do rather than on what we *ought* to do), we will often find excuses to avoid doing what is right. This is particularly true of our moral obligations, one of the most challenging areas of moral behaviour. A moral obligation might be defined as an action we know morally we ought to do, but do not really want to do. Kant believes that his ethical theory safeguards this area of morality, and ensures that we will be adequately motivated to carry out our obligations. So Kant's moral theory makes duty and motive the key factors in morality for free and rational beings, such as human beings.

Kant is suspicious of ethical theories such as Aristotle's, which argue that doing the right thing is good not just for its own sake, but for an end. For Aristotle the end of ethical action is happiness, and he defined happiness as an activity of the soul in accordance with reason and virtue. In short, Aristotle links virtue and happiness, and argues that one of the primary reasons to be moral is because it brings happiness overall, both to ourselves and others. Kant would say that this view of human nature is too idealistic, because there are many moral actions that do not seem to be connected with happiness or human fulfilment; for example, moral obligations such as attending to a sick neighbour. Kant thinks that if we link morality too closely to happiness and human fulfilment, we will often be tempted to shirk our moral obligations. We need a theory that safeguards these obligations, and his 'ethics of duty' does this best.

However, Kant does agree with Aristotle that an ethical life should bring happiness *in the end*. And this point becomes the basis of his moral argument for the existence of God. He argues that in order for the moral order to have rational force for human beings, the practice of virtue and a reward for virtuous living must go hand in hand in some way. Virtue and happiness must be distributed in proportion to one another: the more virtue, the more happiness.[13] This is the only way a rational being can understand the objective moral order as making sense. Although for Kant there can be different motivations for our ethical behaviour, of which duty has to be the main one, the *ultimate* motivation for our belief in an objective moral order has to be that moral practice brings with it some kind of reward, in the form of happiness. Another way to put this is to say that there must be some realm of ultimate justice in the moral order, a realm where virtuous behaviour is rewarded and immoral behaviour is punished, where a correct judgement is made on the actions of Hitler and Lincoln, for example. However, Kant points out, in this life virtue and happiness are manifestly not distributed equally; it is obvious that the moral life does not guarantee happiness or justice in our lifetimes, at least not for many people. And there are plenty of ordinary everyday moral situations, which we all find ourselves in from time to time, where it often seems that it would simply be easier to do the wrong thing, and bring less hassle on ourselves. So why should we do the right thing? Kant's answer is that in order for the whole enterprise of morality to make sense, we have to will (or 'postulate') a proper relationship between virtue and happiness, and this involves willing that objective morality is grounded in the existence of God. As he puts it, 'It is morally necessary to assume the existence of God.'[14] Only if there is a realm where virtue and happiness are distributed proportionally – where the moral life is rewarded and brings happiness and justice – can living according to objective moral values be regarded as rational. If we do not come to see that God is the ground of the objective moral order, the moral order will lack justification, and this lack of justification will eventually affect our moral behaviour for the worse.

It is important to emphasize that Kant is not saying that if we want to believe in objective moral values we should pretend that God exists so that the objective moral order appears to be rational, allowing us to have adequate motivation for our moral behaviour. He is saying that because we are committed to objective moral values as the most rational way to live, we *must* believe in an objective lawgiver as the ultimate source of these values. The argument is straightforward: since belief in, and commitment to, an objective moral order is completely rational, and indeed unavoidable, then God must exist. So although, paradoxically perhaps, Kant was critical of both the cosmological and ontological arguments, he was a supporter of natural theology, and offered this moral argument for the existence of God.

Kant's argument can be stated in a somewhat more general way, a way that does not require one to accept his specific moral theory. The general argument says that in order to believe and practise objective moral values, in order to have an objective moral order, it is necessary to have an objective *ground* for these values, and the existence of God is the best way to ground or justify the moral order. Looking at the matter from the other way around, we might say that the best explanation for the objective moral order is that it was planned out by God and put in place during the creation. We cannot have, the argument continues, laws without a lawgiver, moral values without a judge, fairness and justice in the moral order without an ultimate arbiter. The cosmos, as C.S. Lewis argued, is the kind of place that clearly has an objective moral order, and so this suggests an absolute Being who is the foundation of this moral order.[15] Other explanations can perhaps be given for the objective moral order, and we will look at some of these momentarily, but supporters of the moral argument hold that theism is the *best* explanation for them, a more convincing explanation than any naturalistic, or secularist, alternative. The whole enterprise of morality is very difficult for human beings to make sense of, to justify and to live by, if there is no final justice in this order. The only way there can be final justice is, as Kant indicated, if God exists and is the ultimate source of this moral order.

The argument that theism is the best overall explanation for objective moral values is not one which should be underestimated. This argument is based on the logical pattern of reasoning called inference to the best explanation. This pattern of reasoning is based on asking what, taking all of the evidence together, is probably the best or most likely explanation for a given phenomenon. Philosophers of religion often use this reasoning to develop what has become known as a cumulative case argument for the existence of God. The strategy of the cumulative case argument is that it is one thing to look at the arguments individually, where we see that many of them have merit, but when we take all of these reasonable arguments *together* the case for the existence of God becomes much stronger. Many lines of reasoning point to the existence of God, the theist holds, and they all reinforce each other with cumulative effect, as it were. Some philosophers apply this general strategy to the moral argument, and hold that, given the other arguments for the existence of God, especially the cosmological and design arguments which independently point to an intelligent, ultimate cause of the universe, then it is even more likely that there is an ultimate lawgiver. And this is why we have an objective moral order, and why an objective moral order seems a natural part of the universe. There seems to be a natural relationship, in short, between the existence of God and the existence of objective morality. There may well be other explanations one could offer for the existence of objective morality, but the existence of God, the theist argues, is the best explanation.

One can criticize the moral argument for the existence of God by claiming that there are in fact no objective moral standards at all, no objective moral order, and so there is nothing to ground in the existence of God. Friedrich Nietzsche (1844–1900) argued along these lines that human beings are bundles of desires and drives, and that those who are the strongest or the most powerful will have the most success in promoting their own subjective moral values. And even if many people have acted, and still act, as if there are objective moral standards – holding, say, the view that murder is objectively immoral – they are wrong about this. Versions of this argument have been advanced from time to time, but Nietzsche, like many modern thinkers who speak as if they reject morality altogether, often contradicted himself by occasionally making objective moral judgements! The acceptance of any version of moral relativism, or even moral scepticism, would be a high price to pay in order to block the moral argument. While this is not the place to have a detailed debate about moral relativism vs. moral objectivism, it is true that moral relativism is afflicted with serious problems that make it an unattractive theory for most people. Although many use the language of relativism today, and many young people especially flirt with the theory, few actually hold and practise it as the correct philosophical account of morality. This is because it is not possible to criticize the moral views of others if you are a moral relativist, nor is it possible to support moral progress, or moral reformers. So I think it is true to say that few will defend moral relativism in order to block the moral argument. It seems that belief in and commitment to objective morality is here to stay, and so the existence of an objective moral order needs an explanation.

Some thinkers will attempt to offer a different ground for objective morality than the existence of God, and God's moral plan for humanity. Modern secularists tend to take the view that objective moral values can be justified in some naturalistic way, though there are few, if any, detailed accounts of what this explanation would look like. They may attempt to ground objective moral values in the existence of human nature, for example. Human nature may be defined as a set of traits and characteristics that all human beings share, that are not merely biological, and that have special relevance for morality. These traits might include reason and free will, moral virtues, the need to develop moral character in a certain way, and the need for human relationships. It would, therefore, involve an appeal to an objective moral structure that would be shared by all human beings. Aristotle's ethical theory is largely based on this understanding of human nature. Indeed, this is one of the reasons why Thomas Aquinas found Aristotle's ethical theory attractive, because it provided a way to justify a rich objective moral order without necessarily founding it on religious belief. So this seems to be a way of justifying objective moral values without needing to appeal to an eternal lawgiver.

Yet there are two problems associated with this way of defending objective morality that modern atheists and secularists must face. First, the concept of human nature has undoubted religious connotations, because we would still have to deal with the important question of where we got our human nature. And the usual answer to this question from philosophers who have defended the idea is that we get it from God. God created human beings with a certain nature, just as God created all kinds of life with specific natures. This is what it means to say, in part, that human beings are made in God's image. It seems reasonable to think that any common nature that human beings share must have an explanation, and that this explanation will involve a Creator. So we may be back where we started! Even if one insists on a strictly atheistic reading of Aristotle's account of human nature, his view still crucially appeals to the notion of *teleology* in nature, a notion that later became part of the design argument, and a notion with which modern secularism has considerable difficulty.

This leads us to the second problem. It is difficult for modern secularists to defend morality by an appeal to human nature, because a purely naturalistic, scientific account of reality, and of the existence of life, including human life, seems to leave no room for the existence of human nature. This approach typically eliminates the concept of teleology completely from the story of life, and appeals to Darwinism (understood as a natural process driven purely by chance and random events, as we will see in Chapter 7) as being responsible for the existence, and especially the *nature,* of species. This means that the specific nature a particular species ends up with (say human beings) is due to chance, and not design. This may make it harder for the secularist to argue that there is anything absolutely necessary, anything really objective, about our moral values. In short, if one believes that human beings are purely the product of random, naturalistic processes, it is hard to argue that there is anything *essential* or *necessary* about our nature, and so harder to argue that this nature can be the basis of objective morality. As Charles Taliaferro has observed, 'In a theistic cosmos, values lie at the heart of reality, whereas for most naturalists values are emergent, coming into being from evolutionary processes that are themselves neither inherently good or bad.'[16]

Are there any other alternatives? One might try to ground morality in the good will of human beings, but we saw that this concept eventually led Kant back to the existence of God. We could try to ground objective morality in a doctrine of natural rights in the manner of Locke and the American founding fathers, while denying their further point – that these natural rights come from God. Whether or not you think the moral argument is convincing will depend partly on whether you think alternative attempts at grounding objective morality are likely to be successful. The supporter of the argument thinks that other alternatives are not promising, and that this is why the moral argument is a plausible argument for believing in God.

THE ARGUMENT FROM MIRACLES

It is probably true that many people's reason for believing that God exists is based primarily on their belief that God has performed miracles. These people's concept of miracles can encompass many quite different sorts of event. For instance, some might turn to a life of prayer because they believe that God performed a miracle in curing them of an illness; others might think that it was not an accident that they became a philosopher, or a nurse, or a politician; others might be thankful that they were not hurt in a car wreck. Many such incidents, big and small, surrounding a person's life are often responsible for creating an appreciation for what we might call the experience of the miraculous, and an individual will often regard this as a kind of evidence for the existence of God. Many of the religions of the world also place a strong emphasis on miracles as part of their overall worldview. The argument from miracles, more formally stated, says that certain types of miracles occur in our experience, and that the existence of God is the best explanation for these events.

While we have given several examples of what kinds of event people often regard as miracles, it is important when thinking about this argument to be clear on what we mean by a miracle. A miracle is usually defined in the philosophical debate about miracles as an occurrence of an event that is outside the laws of physics, or that does not seem to obey the normal laws of physics, or that cannot be explained in terms of the laws of physics (or laws of nature), and, further, that the event in question likely has a supernatural cause. This was the definition proposed by David Hume.[17] This is a broad definition and would include, if such events actually happened, the parting of the Red Sea, the resurrection of Jesus, the religious experiences of St Francis of Assisi and God answering our prayers.

It may also include the creation of the universe, since, if we take it that the laws of physics were initiated with the first event in the universe (the Big Bang, say), then the creation itself would be outside the laws of physics. We sometimes understand the concept of a miracle in a narrower sense as well, to include only those events which cannot be explained by the laws of physics, *and* which have some kind of religious significance for the lives of human beings. Understood in this more restrictive sense, the creation of the universe might not count as a miracle, but the resurrection of Jesus would and so would one's belief that one's prayers had been answered.

But some philosophers, such as R.F. Holland, have disputed the claim that miracles must involve a violation of the laws of physics. Holland gives the well-known example of a child wandering out onto train tracks. The driver just happens to faint at the corner before the train comes upon the child, falls on the brake, stopping the train just before it would have killed the child. Holland argues that the *timing* of this event is what should properly be seen as the miracle, even though there was no supernatural intervention.[18] Perhaps we can further add to Holland's example the fact that, in cases like this one, God may have caused the fainting of the driver to occur in a natural way, and so upon examination, his fainting would appear to have a scientific explanation. These examples are intriguing, and would allow us to count as miraculous many events that do not appear to violate the laws of physics.

But if we agree to leave aside Holland's definition for now, the earlier definitions would rule out many events which we often find it hard not to regard as miracles. For example, if you are in a car accident and are not hurt, you might describe this as miraculous, especially if most people in similar types of crashes are hurt. But as long as no violation of the laws of physics is involved it would not be a miracle in the religious sense; it would just be a lucky coincidence. Many of the passengers in the Air France plane crash in Toronto (August 2005) undoubtedly interpreted their survival as a miracle; but it would not qualify under the above definition, because the laws of physics were not violated. The plane was hit by lightning just as it landed, it overshot the runway, did not hit any significant obstacles, and so did not break up, and all of the passengers were able to disembark before the plane caught fire. A narrow escape to be sure, but nothing in this causal story of the crash suggests anything that violates the laws of physics.

So the question is: do miracles, understood as events or happenings outside the laws of physics, occur? The theist claims that they do. It is true that of all the miracles that have been claimed in history, some are undoubtedly fakes, delusions, mistakes, or frauds; but the key point, according to the theist, is that not all of them are. Of course, miraculous claims should be judged on a case-by-case basis, but the theist argues that there are many events for which there is no natural explanation. This may mean that we have not found the natural explanation yet, or it may mean that the event is so unusual that it is not reasonable to think we will find a natural explanation. This is how one might react to one's recovery from a serious illness, after praying to Padre Pio, for example. There are countless cases, in the area of medicine alone, of apparently miraculous events that suggest divine intervention in nature.

Critics of the argument from miracles argue that it is not feasible to believe in miracles in a world dominated by scientific and technological progress, a world where causal explanations are becoming dominant in our approach to the explanations of events in nature. Even some theologians, such as Rudolf Bultmann, have proposed this view. They hold that miraculous claims are indeed always mistakes, or frauds, or delusions, or worse, that there is no possible way to rule out a naturalistic explanation; all we can say at best is that we have not yet found the naturalistic explanation. It is also possible that we will never find it, but it is still the case that in principle there is a naturalistic explanation.

What are we to make of this kind of debate? It is clear that there is a personal aspect and a general, more abstract side to the debate about miracles. The evidence for miracles consists usually of eyewitness testimony, or of a direct experience of a miracle. Hume argued that it was never reasonable to believe in miracles, because one could always question the eyewitness testimony, which was usually offered by people who were very impressionable. He does not appear to have considered the option that one might believe that one had experienced a miracle oneself. A person who believes that she has been the subject of a miraculous event, or perhaps that she has witnessed such an event, will find it hard to take the arguments of the naysayers seriously. On the other hand, those who have not experienced what look like miraculous events personally will be less likely to be convinced. And is Hume right that it is always rational to doubt the testimony of eyewitness reports, such as those reporting the resurrection of Jesus, or the claims of miraculous cures at Lourdes? Are those offering such testimony always impressionable people who are, therefore, unreliable? This does not seem to be the correct response in every case. Surely it must depend on one's best judgement as to how good the eyewitness testimony (and other evidence) is? Many scholars, for example, have looked at evidence supporting the resurrection of Jesus, and concluded that all in all it is rational to believe in this miraculous event because of the evidence.[19] But atheists, such as Michael Martin, disagree. Martin thinks that the evidence for the resurrection is not persuasive, but that even if it were persuasive, it would be more reasonable to think that some (currently undiscovered) natural laws probably brought it about.[20] This debate is hard to settle, but it does seem wrong to rule out by definition, as Hume and others try to do, the possibility of these events providing evidence for miracles. Every person has to look at *specific* claims of the miraculous and make an informed judgement as to whether they are reasonable or not to believe.

Perhaps a general study of miracles would be of benefit here to people thinking about the question. Theists have often been critical of atheistic critiques on this matter because of the tendency of the atheist, or of those sceptical of the possibility of the miraculous, to work with the *assumption* that miracles cannot occur, with little or no discussion of individual cases. The theist insists that while we must not be too credulous, and should maintain a healthy scepticism, one simply cannot rule out the existence of miracles on an *a priori* assumption of naturalism, because this would amount to a begging of the question at issue. A more general point about the argument from miracles is that the miraculous is an intriguing dimension of human experience that requires an explanation. And if one is not inclined to rule out every miraculous claim as false or delusional, then perhaps the realm of the (apparently) miraculous would have a place as part of the cumulative case for the existence of God. In addition, if one has independent reason to believe in God, such as from some of the other arguments we have been considering, then this fact might make the possibility of miracles occurring in nature more likely. Alvin Plantinga has suggested that we should not assume that the rule is that God hardly ever, if at all, interferes in nature, for perhaps it is the case that God regularly interferes in nature.[21] Where one stands on this latter point will depend on one's overall assessment of the evidence for or against theism.

CHAPTER 4

WHAT IS GOD LIKE?

The question of the nature of God – what God is like – has been a source of endless fascination, not just for philosophers but for religious believers of all denominations. Many believers will agree that God exists, but they will often disagree in their conceptions of what God is like, though many of these conceptions will have strong similarities as well. But such questions as: how is God related to the world?; is God a person?; is God omnipotent?; and does God need human beings? have occupied philosophers for centuries, and most major religions have taken official positions on these and related matters concerning the nature of God. Although the existence of God is obviously a fundamental question from the point of view of the rationality of religious belief, it is no less so with the question of the nature of God. In fact, perhaps the latter question is more directly important and relevant for the average religious believer who often does not doubt the existence of God in any serious way, but who must give some thought to the kind of God she is praying to, relies upon and trusts in. One must have some conception of God – as a religious believer and even as an atheist – even if one could not give a philosophical overview or defence of one's conception. The nature of God is a very large topic; we can do no more here that scratch the surface, with the aim of whetting the reader's appetite for further reading and reflection.[1] In this chapter, we will discuss various conceptions of God that have been prominent in western philosophy and theology, occasionally contrasting them with views of God to be found in eastern religions. Along the way we will discuss some of the attributes God is typically thought to possess, such as perfection, omnipotence and omniscience, what they mean, and what problems they might face.

THE CLASSICAL VIEW OF GOD

Let us begin by introducing the classical view of God. This view of God has its origins in Plato and Aristotle, was developed by St Augustine and St Thomas Aquinas, and eventually became dominant in western philosophy and theology. This is the main view of God to be found in Christianity, Judaism and Islam. Although these traditions often have different names for God, and may not agree on every attribute of God, they are largely operating with the same conception of God in their theologies. Indeed, it was only fairly recently that the classical view of God came to be challenged within the western tradition.

In classical theism (or traditional theism), God is conceived of as the Creator of the universe and of all life. He is the ultimate cause of the universe, which he created out of nothing (*ex nihilo*). This was the conclusion arrived at by proponents of the earlier arguments we considered for the existence of God. God is also regarded by classical theists as the sustainer of the world. This means that the world would not remain in existence even for a second if God withdrew his sustaining power, because contingent things do not have the power to keep themselves in existence. God not only creates them, but also keeps them in existence – all created things, animate and inanimate. God is also conceived of in classical theism as an eternal being, as we have seen in Aquinas's version of the cosmological argument especially. This means that God always existed and always will exist. An eternal being is not a contingent being who just happens to exist forever; rather, God is conceived of as a being who exists outside the order of contingent nature altogether.

The classical view of God proposes that God in his own being is immaterial, a personal being, a being who is perfect, omnipotent, omniscient and worthy of worship. Thomas Aquinas argued that we must speak of God analogically, and not equivocally or univocally. This means that we can compare God to human beings in some respects, like saying that God exists or that God is a personal being, but we must recognize that God does not exist and is not a personal being in the same way that you or I exist, or are personal beings. This is the best way to talk about God, because it allows us to speak analogically of his attributes by comparing them to our attributes, while recognizing that they are of a fundamentally different order than the attributes of human beings.[2] Classical theists have also approached the question of the nature of God by means of negative theology (*via negativa*) – the attempt to describe God in terms of what he is not rather than in terms of what he is. For instance, we could say that God is not ignorant, without saying how much knowledge he possesses, or in what way he possesses it; similarly, we can say that God is uncreated to show that he is not a contingent being, without specifying exactly what it means to be an eternal being, because this latter concept is beyond human comprehension. This way one can still talk meaningfully of God, and learn something philosophically about what God is like, while appreciating that God exists in a different way and in a different order to that of the contingent order. Let us elaborate further on some of these attributes of God as a way of enhancing our understanding of the classical view. Later we will contrast this conception of God with more recent views.

Classical theists have argued that God is a perfect being, which means that he is immutable, and does not change. God is understood to be perfect in every way, including morally perfect. Classical theists defend this view by arguing that our world can only contain the phenomenon of change if the Creator of the world is perfect. This is because if God changed in tandem with changes in the world, then God would be *part* of the world, and we would not be able to explain (ultimately) the change that occurs in the world. This argument applies not only to changes in God's essential being, or in God's knowledge, but also to changes in God's moral nature. Another way to express this point is to say that human beings contain their attributes because of their existence. Being, as Thomas Aquinas argued, is the basis of all perfections, and since human beings have limited being, then we would only have our perfections in a limited way. But an unlimited, infinite, eternal being, a being whose essence is supposed to be his existence, would have these perfections in the highest possible way. It is also because God is perfect that we think that he is worthy of worship; if we conceive of God as in any way less than perfect, it gets harder to see why we should give him the total devotion that is at the heart of most of the world's religions.[3]

God is sometimes described by classical theists as being existence itself, and, as we have noted, they hold that it follows from this that God must be absolutely perfect. This classical view is influenced by Aristotle's metaphysics, which made a great impression on Thomas. Aristotle argued that only that which has matter can change; further, anything made up of matter is made up of parts, and the existence of the parts coming together in a certain way to form an object requires some principle which must be outside the parts. He developed this view to argue that objects in the world exist (or have actuality), and can change (can develop their potentiality). In this way, he explained existence and change in the universe by means of the concepts of actuality (existence) and potentiality (change). Aristotle (and Thomas followed him in this) then applied this thinking to the nature of God to argue that God must be 'pure act', which means pure actuality. This means that God has no matter, and so has no potential, and so is perfect. He is fully actual, in short. This thinking also confirms that God must be an immaterial being, because if he were a material being he would be a contingent being, and so would need a cause, which would compromise his perfection. Classical theists further developed this Aristotelian analysis to argue that God is simple, which means that God does not have parts in himself. They believed this was the case, because if God had parts in himself it would mean that he was made of matter, and some principle would be required – a principle outside God – to explain how the parts in God come together in one being, just as we need a principle to explain how the parts in a physical object come together to form the object. God's various attributes on this view are just different ways of expressing his nature, which is simple and perfect.[4] This is an intriguing argument for the simplicity of God, but it is one that has been challenged today.

This overview of the classical approach to the nature of God makes it clear that on this view God is perfect in every sense, including in the moral sense, which means that he has the attribute of omnibenevolence. This is to say that God is a necessarily good being in a *metaphysical* sense – a being in the highest possible, indeed in a perfect, moral state – because he always chooses what is right even though he could do otherwise (because he is also a free being). However, if we accept this view of God, some apparently unusual conclusions follow. One is that God does not need human beings. If this is true, it would follow that God did not create human beings because he needed to, say because he needed our love and companionship, or because he wanted to look after us, because all of these things imply that God lacks something, and had to create us to fulfil this lack. But if God lacks something, then God is not perfect. Another conclusion that follows is that God is not capable of emotion. This again is because to display emotion, say joy or sorrow at the actions of human beings, is to imply a lack in God. If God were to respond with joy to the return of the prodigal son (as his father did), then it would follow that God has been fulfilled in some way, which again implies that God is not perfect. It also follows from this view of God that God cannot feel suffering or pain, and that he does not suffer himself. This is not just because he is an immaterial being; it is also because to feel sorrow, like we do, means that there are situations that are outside his control and that cause him pain – say a particular human being fails to respond in the right way to a challenge and God thereby feels sorrow – then this implies that he is imperfect in some sense. A being who feels sorrow at an event is thereby moved by the event and this is not compatible with God's perfection, because it would follow from this that God could be significantly affected by what we do on earth, could be worried, sorrowful or happy, all of which imply that he is presently unfulfilled and subject to the vagaries of human actions and events, just as we are.

For classical theists, God is so beyond human understanding that it is difficult for us to grasp what God is like. The more we think we have an understanding of what God is like, or the more we think that God is a very glorified version of human beings, the more wrong we are likely to be. This is why classical theists employ negative theology to describe God. In saying what God is not – not like us in various respects – we can attempt to give some insight into what God is like. So a classical theist will say that God thinks, wills, causes, hopes, loves and so on, but is careful to stress that these concepts are not to be understood in God in the same way we would understand them in human beings. The argument here is straightforward. God cannot love in the same way that we can love, for example, because our kind of love involves change and emotion, but God is not subject to change and emotion. In addition, love in human beings seems to require as a necessary condition the fact that human beings be embodied beings, but again God is not embodied, so it follows that God's love is different from human love. The same is true for God coming to know something. For us to know something is to use our senses and reasoning, but God has no senses and so would not come to knowledge this way. Also, since God is all-knowing, it is not clear that he ever comes to know anything about the world; that is to say, he may not come to gain any new knowledge. It may not be possible for him to discover anything which he does not already know, an issue we will come back to later in our discussion of omniscience.

According to classical theists, God is a personal God, but again we have to be careful to note that he is not a person in the sense in which you and I are persons. This is because human persons belong to a certain type of species, are embodied and have various necessary attributes, none of which God has in an identical sense. God is not embodied, and is unique in terms of his kind. So classical theists adopt the view that, given that God is perfect, immaterial, all-knowing and all-powerful, all of these other points about the nature of God follow logically, and that if one gives them up, or rejects them, so one must explain how one will deal with the problems that would result. For example, if one were to say that God's love is essentially similar to human love, one would have to explain how this could be, given that God is immaterial and perfect.

CHALLENGES TO THE CLASSICAL VIEW

Various contemporary philosophers are unhappy with some aspects of the classical view of God, and have challenged it on a number of grounds.[5] One problem that has worried many in theology as well as philosophy is the view that God does not change, that God does not suffer or experience emotion, that God does not need human beings. Contemporary philosophers and theologians are uncomfortable with this conception of God for two reasons. First, they argue that it would be hard to understand and make sense of God's relationship to human beings if one does not hold that God's nature is subject to at least some forms of change. For example, the activity of prayer seems to require not only that God hears our prayers, but that at least sometimes he is moved by them, and decides to respond to them. But if God responds to our prayers, surely this means that some change occurs in God? The same is true of our seeking God's forgiveness. Surely if God responds to our request for forgiveness, this must mean that God is disappointed in us, listens to our appeals, and decides to forgive us, all of which seems to require that God's nature undergo change. Similarly, some critics of the classical view argue that the fact that one of God's attributes is love is hard to reconcile with the idea that God does not change, because surely the essence of love, at least as we understand it, requires that the individuals who love each other do change in various ways, by becoming happier, more fulfilled, more concerned, and so on. Would it not be the same in God, even if we agree that we are speaking analogically of God's nature, even if we acknowledge that God's love is not fully the same as human love? And, more generally, would it not be the case that as human beings move closer to God, God would become more fulfilled because his creation is responding to him, in the same way that a parent would be fulfilled when their children at last begin to appreciate them? Would God not be sorrowful if his creation moved away from him? Indeed, the parent/child analogy is one that modern thinkers often adopt to describe God's relationship to his creatures.

The second reason some modern thinkers believe that God must undergo change in his relationship with human beings is that this seems to be what is required *morally* if our relationship with God is to make sense. This is a point emphasized by thinkers in the movement known as process theism, in particular. Process theism is influenced by process philosophy, a movement based on the thought of Alfred North Whitehead. The main concepts in Whitehead's thought were applied to religious topics by Charles Hartshorne, who proposed the view that reality is not static, but is in process, and that, therefore, God is best understood as having a dynamic, even organic, relationship with his creation.[6] There is a back and forward between God and the world, and God, as well as his creation, develops in this relationship. Process theists argue that God, as conceived of in the classical view, seems too remote, too hard to relate to, and this remoteness would make it difficult to sustain religious life and practice. It is hard to see how we could pray to God or not be intimidated by God if we adopted the classical conception. The claim is that for God to able to respond to us in a *morally appropriate* way God has to be the kind of being that would undergo change. Hartshorne thinks, for example, that we would not admire a God who was unaffected by human suffering. These sorts of criticisms of the classical view of God are often motivated by our intuitions about the kind of God we would like to believe in, by our requirements for what God should be like. But the classical theists argue that our intuitions about what God should be like might not be a good guide to the nature of God; they hold that a God who does not need humans but who still creates us and provides for our salvation is more perfect than a God who does need humans and who creates us partly to fulfil his own need. The classical theists reject the view of French thinker Emmanuel Levinas, who suggested that the reason that God created human beings was because he was lonely and needed somebody to talk to! It is also worth mentioning that in this dispute between the classical theists and the process theists both sides often appeal to the Bible for support; indeed support for both points of view can be found in the Bible. Some theists, such as Bernard of Clairvaux (1090–1153), and, in our own time, Richard Swinburne, have tried to respond to the claim that God is too remote by reminding us that God became incarnate, in the person of Jesus Christ, so that he might share human suffering.

Some of the traditional attributes of God, such as omnipotence and omniscience, have in themselves been the subject of much recent discussion, and it is to this discussion that we must now turn.

GOD'S OMNIPOTENCE

God has traditionally been thought of as an omnipotent being. There are various reasons for attributing omnipotence to God. The first is that this is what is required by perfection, an attribute we have already looked at. Classical theists argue that a perfect being would also be an omnipotent being because he would have to be a being who could do anything that it is logically possible to do, otherwise he would not be a perfect being. Their view is that it is hard to conceive of God as a being limited in power, because this would seem to reduce God to the status of a being who would be alongside the universe, rather than the creator of the universe. Some contemporary philosophers, notably Richard Swinburne, have suggested that a being who created the universe would have to be a very powerful being indeed, and that the simplest explanation of his power is to say that he is an omnipotent being. If we conceive of God as a limited being, Swinburne says, we run into all sorts of problems concerning the being who created the universe, like, for instance, whether he would be limited in the type of universe he could have created, or whether he would be subject to external influence, so the simplest explanation is that God is omnipotent.[7] Thirdly, this conception of God is also consistent with what the Bible says about God.[8]

However, the concept of omnipotence is a quite difficult concept to understand, and we need to look further at some of the issues raised by it. Let us begin with the view of Thomas Aquinas.[9] Thomas argued that to say that God is omnipotent does not mean what many typically take it to mean – that God can do anything. It means only that God can do whatever it is logically possible to do. The notion of logical possibility is an important one in philosophy. It refers to whatever can be done *without contradiction*; this does not mean necessarily that it will be done, but only that it could be done. So on this understanding of logical possibility, it would be logically possible for me to learn Chinese but not for me to discover how to square the circle, because the latter task implies a contradiction, and is not logically possible. Applying this notion to God, Thomas argues that there are two sets of actions that even an omnipotent being like God cannot do. The first set covers things that are straightforwardly logically contradictory, such as squaring the circle, or, as we will see later in the discussion of the problem of evil, creating free beings that God can nevertheless ensure *always* choose good over evil. So an omnipotent being cannot do what is logically contradictory. As Thomas puts it: 'God is unable to make opposites exist in the same subject at the same time and in the same respect.'[10] Yet there is still more that God cannot do.

Thomas introduces an interesting second set of actions which he believes God cannot do. These all relate to actions that are incompatible with God's nature. Thus, Thomas argues that God cannot sin, cannot be angry, that he cannot create a being equal to himself, that God cannot repent, or will anything evil. God would not be God, for instance, if he were to will to commit a sin, or if he were to commit a sin: he would no longer retain his perfect moral nature. Nor would he be God if he were really angry at mankind, on Thomas's view; this would also compromise his perfection. Now the question arises as to whether God cannot perform these actions because of necessity, or simply because he freely chooses not to perform them. In other words, does God not sin because he cannot sin, is morally incapable of sin, or is it because he can sin, but simply will not sin? Augustine seemed to argue that God by nature cannot sin (which seems to mean *necessarily* cannot sin), whereas later thinkers such as Samuel Clarke (1675–1729) held that: 'God always discerns and approves what is just and good, necessarily, and cannot do otherwise: But he always acts or does what is just and good freely; that is, having at the same time a full natural or physical power of acting differently.'[11] This means that God necessarily sees what is right (and always does it), but is free to do what is wrong. Clarke's interpretation is attractive to theists because we tend to think that God's moral goodness requires that he be free. This is because an all-good being who cannot help being good is, to our intuition at least, not as perfect as an all-good being who can help being good. In short, a being who always does what is right because he cannot do otherwise is not as good as a being who could do evil if he wanted to but never does! So to say that God is omnipotent on this understanding should not be taken to include saying that God cannot do evil, or cannot sin. God may be able to do these things but will not do them. This is because God is good in an absolute or metaphysical sense, meaning that God is God – a being in a perfect moral state – because he always chooses what is right even though he could do otherwise.

This brings us to what is sometimes called the paradox of the stone.[12] This is the paradox generated by the question: can God create a stone that is too heavy for him to lift? If God is omnipotent, then he should be able to create a stone of any weight, and so should be able to create one that is too heavy to lift. So lifting this stone would be something that he cannot do. If God cannot make the stone, then he is not omnipotent, since an omnipotent being should be able to make a stone of any weight. Some philosophers raise this problem not just to explore the matter of what it is logically possible for God to do, but to suggest that the concept of omnipotence is itself contradictory. Theistic philosophers typically reply to this point by arguing that this is a contradictory action we are expecting God to do; since it is contradictory it is really no challenge to the claim that God is omnipotent. It is contradictory because God can lift a stone of any size whatsoever, but we are then asking him to create a stone that he cannot lift. Since this is a contradiction, the paradox dissolves. This solution assumes that God is omnipotent. Yet, if we understand the paradox as asking whether God is omnipotent or not, rather than as generating a paradox for an omnipotent God, i.e. if we look as the paradox as saying that omnipotence itself makes no sense, then this reply to it is not perhaps quite adequate. Another way of looking at the problem is to agree that God can make such a stone, but deny that it challenges the notion of omnipotence, because it can be said that the reason God cannot lift the stone is *because* of his omnipotence. In short, it is because God is omnipotent that we can have this kind of stone in the first place (and so can generate our paradox), so we cannot conclude from the paradox so generated that God is not omnipotent because he cannot lift the stone. We *can* conclude, though, that an omnipotent being is not a being who can do absolutely anything. But we have already seen this above – an omnipotent being, according to theists, is limited in what he can do to what is logically possible, and by what is consistent with his own nature.

GOD'S OMNISCIENCE

Theists also typically hold that God is omniscient. This is another attribute that we can know analogically of God, and that is also required by his perfection. But what does it mean to say that God is omniscient? After our discussion of omnipotence, we should probably be wary of concluding that it means that God knows absolutely everything. Would an omniscient God know everything there is to know about the universe, and about human beings? Would he know all of our thoughts, plans, and even our futures? One way to place a limit on what an omniscient being could know would be to say that, as with omnipotence, an omniscient God knows everything that it is logically possible for him to know. But what does this class of propositions include? Does it include future actions that God himself might do? Perhaps not. God may not know what he is going to do in the future until he decides what to do, so it would be no failing of an omniscient being that he does not know what he is going to do in the future long before he does it. God's own freedom would seem to require that he does not know what he is going to do in the future. But what about future *human* actions? This brings us to what is known as the problem of God's foreknowledge and human freedom.

This problem is predicated on the question of whether an omniscient being could know all future human actions? If he does, then how can it be that human beings are really free? And if he does not, does this mean that he may lose control of the universe, in the sense that he does not know how his plans for human salvation are going to turn out. Let us state the problem more clearly. It would seem that if God is omniscient, then he would know all future human actions. He would know, for example, that in three years' time you are going to get a new job, or get married, or have a son. But if God truly knows this, then it has to happen, it must necessarily come about that you get the new job, or get married, or have a son. But if this is the case, then it would seem to follow that at that time in the future when, for instance, you are presented with the offer of the new job, you are not really free to reject the job. If you reject the job, then this means that God is wrong to think that you were going to take the job, and so is not omniscient. On the other hand, if you must neces-sarily take the job, then it seems that you do not have a genuinely *free* choice as to whether or not to take it. This problem requires that we think of God as being *in time*, so that at the present time he knows something that is going to happen at a future time, yet at that future time (when you are thinking about whether or not to take the job) you are supposed to be able to choose freely whether to take the job. So if God knows at the earlier time that you are going to take the job, but at the later time when you freely reject the job, your free action means that God has a false belief about the future. So it would seem that God's omniscience is not compatible with human freedom.

One solution to this problem is to accept that God does not know the future. This would solve the problem, because we would simply recognize that it is not logically possible for an omniscient being to know the future actions of free human beings. Just as the genuine freedom of human beings precludes *our* knowing what human beings will do in the future, this is also true of God. The only way that God could know for certain what we were going to do would be for him to program us, and this would mean that we would not be free. However, we must note that if God does not know the future, then this is a limitation that God has placed on himself in the sense that God has created free human beings knowing that he would not be able to know what future actions they might perform, because he has given them free will.

This solution is contentious, because some theists think that it is not obvious that this logical limitation should be placed on God. They argue that even though it is true that *we* cannot know future human actions because human beings are genuinely free, this limit-ation might not apply to God. Perhaps it is logically possible for God to know for certain what X is doing to do in the future, and yet X's decision in the future could still be genuinely free. This might not make sense to our limited way of looking at things, because of our difficulty in understanding what freedom involves. But because God created the universe and human life, and all the conditions for human choices, it might be that he can read with certainty what we are going to do even though we are doing it freely. It is true that the concept of freedom would seem to preclude this, but God's knowl-edge of the universe might be so vast that he can predict with *com-plete certainty* what we will do even though we are doing it freely. It is not clear that this involves a contradiction.

The claim that God does not know the future is contentious for a further reason: it seems to place the final salvation of mankind outside God's control. That is to say, it could be the case that God's creation will freely reject God, and that although God has an elaborate plan for the salvation of man, it could be permanently frustrated by our free choices. Although we will see later that some philosophers (like John Hick, for example) argue that God will take steps to prevent this from occuring, the worry is that if we are genuinely free, God may not be able to do much about it. One way philosophers have tried to deal with these problems is to suggest that God is *outside time* altogether. We saw that the problem of divine foreknowledge and human freedom is generated by the fact that God is said to be in time just as you and I are in time. But what if God is not in time?

This view was held by several classical theists including Boethius, Augustine and Thomas Aquinas.[13] They argued that God is not in time at all. This is what it means in part to say that God is eternal. If this view is correct, it would mean that God would not experience the universe from moment to moment as human beings do, as a series of consecutive events in which there is a 'before' and 'after', as well as a 'present'. He would experience everything that happens in the universe as happening all at once, as a kind of all-encompassing present, where the past and the future are somehow happening all at once as perceived by God's consciousness. Past, present and future are all continually present to God's consciousness. This view is also consistent with the classical argument that God does not change, because if God was in time, it would seem that in experiencing the universe from moment to moment God would have to undergo change. He would come to know things, for example, that he did not know before. This view of God may also find support in modern physics, which suggests that time is linked to change. Although it can be notoriously difficult to get a definition of time, some modern cosmologists have suggested that time came into existence after the Big Bang, and as time passes, change occurs. This view may be a consequence of modern physics, but it does not necessarily follow that time and change are essentially related, though it is a good working hypothesis. But, if true, what then was the situation before God created the universe? Perhaps at that point there was no time understood as a succession of events. Did God undergo change before he created the universe?

In this way, classical theists could appeal to modern physics to support their view that the concept of time only makes sense within the universe. God is outside time, and so there is no problem of divine foreknowledge and human freedom (indeed, if God is outside time in this way, he really does not have *fore*knowledge). Does this solution make sense? Is it intelligible to say that God sees everything in the universe happening all at once? Remember, that this does not just mean that God sees things happening in the universe from some unique 'God's eye' vantage point outside it. If this is all it meant, God would still experience the universe through time. It means that God sees what you did yesterday, what you are doing now and what you will do tomorrow, somehow happening all at once, and this would be true for every event, and for the actions of every human being in the universe throughout history. In this way, God would have complete knowledge of the past, present and future. It is clear to us this not only does not make sense, but seems clearly logically impossible. But our question is: might it be logically possible for God? The classical theists hold that it is because there is such a vast difference between God's existence, power and knowledge and ours, coupled with the fact that God created the universe and our order of time, that we should not rule it out. These theists hold that this is the best way to think of God's relationship to the universe. It is rather like the concept of eternity in this respect. Most theists accept that this is a difficult concept for the human mind to grasp (as we saw in our discussion of Thomas's version of the cosmological argument), yet they would not deny that it is an intelligible way to think about the existence of God. But some modern theists counter that it would be hard to make sense of the notion of forgiveness, for instance, on this view of time because, as noted above, the experience of forgiveness would seem to require a past, present and future.

A NOTE ON EASTERN VIEWS OF GOD

We have noted that in the great Western religions – Judaism, Christianity and Islam – God is conceived as an eternal being who exists independently of the world, who is an intelligent, free agent, who is omnipotent, omniscient and omnibenevolent. This view is in contrast to the view of God often found in the great religions of the east – Hinduism, Buddhism, Confucianism, Taoism, Shinto and others. There is a lot of diversity within these religions concerning the nature of God, and sometimes it can be difficult to speak of the 'Hindu' view of God, for instance, since there is support for more than one view in that tradition. Although some Hindu thinkers do present God as an independent, personal being who is separate from the world (this is the view of God in the *Bhagavad Gita*, for instance), the dominant view of God among Hindu thinkers, especially Shankara (788–820), is that God does not exist as an independent consciousness (this is the view found in the *Upanishads*, for example). The Hindu view of salvation, as developed in the Advaita Vedanta school of Hinduism, involves escaping the cycle of 'samsara'. This involves belief in reincarnation, whereby the individual dies and is reborn in another human body. This cycle of birth, death and rebirth goes on until the purified soul or consciousness escapes into Nirvana. However, Shankara conceives of Nirvana as an entry into total unity with the Godhead, but this is not to be understood in the same way as it would be understood in Christianity, where the individual and God retain their separate identities, and enter into a relationship. This oneness encompasses all reality; there is no separate existence of souls. Our aim, according to Shankara, is to escape the physical world, which is a world of appearances and illusions, to achieve this oneness.

In Hinduism, and in strands of Buddhism, after we escape the cycle we enter into a kind of oneness, where the individual is not really conscious or personal. The individual self is absorbed into the One. This is a monist version of Hinduism, which holds that there is only one reality, not two. This particular view of God is in sharp contrast to the western view discussed in this chapter. But there is another strand in Hinduism which is more comparable to the western view. This is represented by thinkers such as Ramanuja (1017–1137), who seek to retain the distinction between God and creation, and who see God as being an all-powerful being who created the cosmos. On this view God is seen as a parent: loving, merciful, omniscient and almighty. The view of Ramanuja depicts God as a creator, and holds that the universe and human beings are distinct from God.[14]

If we focus on the similarities in conceptions of God in both eastern and western traditions, we can have a debate about the existence of God, the relationship of God to the world, and about the nature of salvation, especially its implications for morality.

However, if we contrast theism with monism, the debate is more strained. Western philosophers in general have been critical of monism on the grounds that it lacks coherence, precisely because the identity of both the individual and of the whole is lost in the notion of absorption. It is hard to see how salvation and the moral life that leads to it can be sustained if one does not retain one's separate identity throughout the process. From the point of view of God's nature, western thinkers hold that God must exist in some independent sense if he is the creator of the universe and of all life, however individual religions come to understand God's creative activity. If this is the case, then God and individual human beings must retain their separate identities throughout the process of salvation. There has also been disagreement between east and west on the nature of immortality, with eastern views long supporting the notion of reincarnation. I will return to the question of the plurality of the world's religions in the last chapter, when I shall have more to say about the eastern religions.

CHAPTER 5

GOD AND EVIL

One of the most vexing problems for many of us, no matter which worldview we happen to subscribe to, is the existence of evil in the world. Whenever we reflect on the overall human condition – the general fate of human beings in the universe – while there are obviously many positive experiences indicative of hope and meaning, nevertheless we all experience the fact of evil in our daily lives. Indeed, it seems to be a significant part of our plight that we have to cope with evil in its various forms over the course of our lives. We have all been touched by the reality of evil in one way or another, and so the question naturally arises: why does evil exist at all? This is a troubling question for everyone, but it appears to be an especially troubling question for religious believers. This is because the religious believer holds that God created the universe and all life for some ultimately good purpose, and so we naturally wonder why God did not create a world free from evil. In addition, the religious believer usually also holds that God is all-powerful, all-good and all-knowing (as we saw in the last chapter). So it seems reasonable to think that if God possesses these attributes that he would have created a world in which there is little or no evil. Isn't this what we should expect to find, given that God has the power to prevent evil, and also given that God has the morally good nature to want to prevent evil? The atheist argues that the existence of evil can form the basis of a strong argument against the existence of God. Indeed, most religious philosophers find 'the problem of evil' argument a far more challenging argument than typical criticisms of the cosmological and design arguments, or criticisms of some of the other arguments we considered in Chapter 3. Pastors and priests will often point out, for instance, that this is one of the most difficult aspects of their work: trying to give comfort to people who have lost loved ones, or suffered other tragedies, trying to explain how a supposedly good God could allow such things to happen. It is true that suffering can sometimes make people believers, or draw them closer to God, but it is also true that suffering can drive people to atheism.

EVIL, AND THE PROBLEM OF EVIL

It can be quite difficult to give a precise definition of evil, so it is best to begin our analysis of the problem of evil by indicating the sorts of things the concept of evil is generally used to describe. Philosophers describe bad events and bad experiences as evil, and these are usually, though not always, associated with human suffering in some way. It is possible to go further and distinguish two categories of evil events, natural and moral. Natural evil refers to evil events that seem to occur naturally in the world such as earthquakes, floods, famines and disease. These events occur naturally but obviously can cause terrible suffering for human beings – witness the horrific tsunami in Asia in 2004. Moral evil refers to the evil actions of human beings, such as murder, rape, torture, robbery, and so forth. The distinction between moral and natural evil is an important one because it seems that natural events are on a different plane than human actions, and yet a solution to the problem of evil would need to explain both kinds of evil.

The problem of evil, as it is usually described in the philosophy of religion, is the problem of how to reconcile the fact of both natural and moral evil with the existence of a God who is supposed to be all-powerful, all-good and all-knowing. As Hume stated the problem, 'Is [God] willing to prevent evil, but not able? Then he is impotent. Is he able but not willing? Then he is malevolent. Is he both able and willing? Whence then is evil?'[1] If God is all-powerful, why does he not prevent evil, and if God is all-good, why would he not want to prevent evil? (And the answer to this problem cannot appeal to any ignorance on God's part of what is going on in the world, because God is generally conceived to be all-knowing as well.) It appears to be logically inconsistent to say, on the one hand, that God is all-powerful and all-good, and yet to say, on the other hand, that evil exists in the world. Two responses that would remove the logical inconsistency are usually immediately ruled out by the religious believer. The first is to say that God is not all-powerful – that God does not have quite enough power to prevent the evil that does occur. Although God would like to stop evil, he cannot. The second response is to say that, although God has enough power to prevent evil, he will not prevent it because he is not all-good; that is, God somehow desires evil! Sometimes this latter point is expressed by noting, not that God desires evil, but that God's ways are not our ways, that God may be operating with some higher form of morality that is beyond the human mind to grasp. But neither of these answers is usually acceptable to the traditional religious believer, because they appear to compromise two of the attributes of God, omnipotence and omnibenevolence. This is why critics of theism who appeal to the problem of evil usually argue that the existence of evil makes it very likely that there is no God at all. In other words, the most likely answer to why God allows evil is that there is no God! It is important to state the atheistic conclusion this way, because to say that evil makes it unlikely that God exists is not the same as saying that the *reason* evil exists is because God does not exist. God's non-existence would not explain *why* evil exists in the world. Even if there is no God, we would still have the fact of evil, and this would still require an explanation.

PROBLEMS OF EVIL: LOGICAL, EVIDENTIAL, EXISTENTIAL

In order to explore the problem of evil further, it is helpful to distinguish between three ways of looking at the problem. The first is called the logical problem of evil, and was famously defended by the British philosopher J.L. Mackie.[2] Mackie claimed that the existence of an all-good and all-powerful God is *logically inconsistent* with the existence of evil in the world. What he means is that if God exists, then evil cannot exist. This is because God is supposed to be all-good, and it seems to follow from this that whatever God makes must be all-good as well, that an all-good being would want to create the best kind of world, would prevent evil if he could. So if evil exists, this would be logically incompatible with the existence of God. So, since evil does exist, God does not. Mackie acknowledges that a typical reply to this argument is that the contradiction, if it is there at all, is not very obvious, because surely God could have some reason for evil. On the face of it, God's existence and the existence of evil do not seem to be logically incompatible. Mackie agrees that the contradiction may not be immediately obvious, but thinks that if we attend carefully to what is actually involved in our idea of God, and to what the existence of evil means, it is reasonable to conclude that God and the existence of evil are logically incompatible. Yet it seems that Mackie has overstepped the mark here, and made too strong a claim. For even when we examine the concepts carefully, it still seems that an all-good, all-powerful God could exist, but have some reason for allowing evil to exist. Just because we do not think we know the reason does not mean that there is no reason. It is hard to see the *logical* incompatibility Mackie is defending.

This has led other philosophers, most notably William Rowe, to develop a different formulation of the problem, called the evidential problem of evil. The evidential problem of evil was perhaps best illustrated in Fyodor Dostoevsky's great novel *The Brothers Karamazov*. In this novel, Ivan Karamazov, a religious believer, raises the problem of evil in the horrifying scene where the general orders the dogs to tear apart the little child in front of his mother, all because the child in question had injured the general's favourite dog. Ivan, a religious believer, suggests that whatever the ultimate reason may turn out to be for evil deeds like this one, he cannot accept it. Ivan is here drawing a distinction, I think, between an *explanation* and a *justification* for the existence of evil. An explanation after all is not always sufficient for justification. And what Ivan Karamazov is suggesting is that perhaps no explanation of God's can justify the behaviour of the general. It is precisely this kind of distinction, I believe, which gives the evidential argument its force, and makes it a strong argument against the existence of God. The evidential argument challenges the theist to explain in a way that *plausibly justifies* why an all-good and all-powerful God would allow terrible evils such as human and animal suffering.

This version of the problem drops Mackie's strong claim that evil and the existence of God are logically incompatible, and argues for a weaker claim: that the existence of evil in the world makes it *unlikely* that God exists. Rowe's restatement of the problem of evil is cleverly constructed. He deliberately does not claim to *prove* that God does not exist, but only that it is *probable* that God does not exist. Rowe employs this argument to propose that it is rational to be an atheist. He also does not go so far as to say that it is irrational to be a theist. Describing himself as a friendly atheist, he simply argues that the existence of evil in the world makes it unlikely or improbable that God exists, and this makes it rational to be an atheist.[3] In a curious way, because he is making these weaker claims, not claiming to prove that God does not exist, and allowing that religious belief might be rational too, some think Rowe actually makes a more plausible case overall for the rationality of atheism.

Before I elaborate Rowe's version of the evidential argument, let me briefly conclude this section by referring to the existential problem of evil. The existential problem refers to the actual fact or experience of evil in a person's life, and how they might cope with it, respond to it, interpret it, and so on. Some philosophers have described the logical and evidential problems of evil as abstract problems, whereas the existential problem is a concrete problem, a problem that affects the lives of real people, and they have suggested that solving the former may not help with the latter, or that perhaps the whole issue should be approached mainly from the existential side. Philosophers of religion are usually concerned only with the abstract problem, but they do argue that if one arrives at a plausible, consistent answer to the abstract problem, this may help one deal with the existential problem. On the other hand, many would also acknowledge that it is one thing to understand, and perhaps accept, in an abstract way why God might allow evil, but quite another thing actually to cope with evil in one's life. But just because there is a clear difference between thinking about evil as an abstract problem and actually dealing with it in real life, it does not follow that one should not engage in the abstract debate, that the abstract debate has no value. The problem of evil in philosophy of religion raises a question that has troubled religious believers, as well as atheists; philosophers, therefore, have a responsibility to think about it carefully, and to try to come to grips with it.

THE EVIDENTIAL PROBLEM OF EVIL

Let us elaborate the evidential problem of evil further, and see how it functions as an argument for the rationality of atheism. William Rowe's argument consists of two straightforward premises. He argues that an omnipotent God *could* prevent evil without losing some greater good, or without permitting some evil equally bad or worse. He also believes that an omnibenevolent God *would* prevent evil unless he could not do so without losing some greater good or permitting some evil equally bad or worse. God's moral nature is all-good, so it is reasonable to think that he would not want evil to occur. The first premise concerns God's all-powerful nature, and the second concerns God's all-good nature. Rowe believes that the second premise is uncontroversial, and so only the first premise needs illustration. Most religious believers will agree that God's nature is such that, if he could, he would want to prevent evil from occurring. God would be at least as decent as a decent human being, and this is what a decent human being would do if she was creating a world, so surely God would do the same.

To illustrate the first premise, therefore, Rowe considers some actual cases of evil, and attempts to illustrate by means of them the kind of power an omnipotent God would have. He believes that we sometimes do not attend in concrete fashion to this point, and often think of omnipotence only in the abstract. To elaborate this point, Rowe concentrates on pain and suffering in the animal kingdom. He uses the well-known illustration of a fawn, who is trapped in a forest fire, and who suffers horribly for several days before eventually dying. Could an omnipotent God have prevented the suffering of the fawn? The answer seems to be yes. Would some greater good have been lost by not stopping the fawn's suffering? No, Rowe argues, because God could bring about the greater good *without* needing the suffering of the fawn to occur. For example, suppose a man walking past the forest on the second or third day of the fawn's suffering hears the fawn crying out, alerts the local people and saves the town from burning down. This would be a case of good coming out of evil, but Rowe argues that God could have saved the town in some other way that did not require the fawn's suffering. Similarly, God could have prevented the fawn's suffering without allowing some greater evil to happen instead, again because he has the power to do so. After all, God is omnipotent.

Rowe does allow that in some cases evil might lead to a greater good. But he questions why God needs the evil to occur at all, if God is all-good and all-powerful. He further adds that, even if we were to allow that some evil is necessary to bring about some greater good, that there is still *too much* natural evil in the world, especially if we include all of the suffering in the animal kingdom. There seem also to be too many cases of *pointless* evil – that is, evil events that seem to be mainly destructive of human well-being and happiness, that do not seem to serve any greater point (sometimes called gratu-itous evil). All of this, Rowe concludes, makes it rational to look at the case of the fawn suffering in the forest (and many similar cases) and to come to the conclusion that there is very likely no God.

Some philosophers have questioned the description of any particular evil event as pointless on the grounds that we would have to know for certain that it was serving no greater purpose in order to know that it was truly 'pointless'. For any given case of evil, perhaps some good might come out of it, and in some cases we might recognize this goodness, and in some cases we might not. For example, take the case of a criminal in a particular city who accidentally kills a person while robbing a bank. The criminal is so devastated at what happens that he reforms and starts an organization to help other criminals in that city make a fresh start. This organization gains momentum and eventually has considerable success in helping many criminals turn away from their evil ways. Over the course of several years, the number of evil incidents related to crime in that particular city will decrease. This seems to be a case of good coming out of evil. Indeed, much of human history is a story of progress of this kind where we have made effective improvements to minimize human suffering by learning from past mistakes. This is a fairly clear-cut case of good coming out of evil, yet it is not clear that it helps us come to terms with the evidential problem of evil.

This is because there are many other cases where we can see no obvious good resulting from an evil occurence. What about all of those cases where evil incidents related to robbery and violence do not seem to produce any good? Rowe's evidential objection asks why God could not have created a world in which incidents like these were minimized, and where those that do occur all have an obvious point to them so that at least we would not come to believe that much evil is pointless. Rowe simply says that it is very reasonable to conclude that there is no reason for this kind of evil (even though we could be wrong). Since it is pointless, and it would make no sense to say that God allows pointless evils, the conclusion that there is no God is rational. Rowe has also emphasized, as we have seen, that an omnipotent God could surely bring about the good without needing the evil events to occur. Further, the evidential objection gets its strength precisely because, unlike with Mackie's logical problem of evil mentioned above, it does not claim to prove that God does not exist. Rowe realizes this would be an unrealistic claim, and would be very difficult to show. So, ironically, in making the more modest claim that the argument only shows that it is likely that God does not exist, his argument may be more persuasive.

THEISTIC REPLIES: THE FREE-WILL DEFENCE

How might the theist reply to various arguments for atheism based on the problem of evil? The response of theistic philosophers usually must include at the very least some general argument stating that God has a reason for evil, but not necessarily saying what that reason is. This approach is called a *defence*. Some philosophers go further and try to offer a theory to explain what God's reasons are for allowing evil. These theories are called *theodicies*, and we will come back to some of them later. One of the best-known forms of defence is called the 'free-will defence'. Proponents of this argument, including St Augustine (354–430) and, more recently, Alvin Plantinga, Michael Peterson and John Hick, argue that the highest gift that God can give to his creatures is free will. This includes the freedom to do what we choose, including rejecting God. But free will comes at a price – it means that human beings can choose evil if they wish. The point is that it is not possible for God always to *prevent* human beings from choosing evil, and yet at the same time ensure that they are fully free beings with a *genuine choice* between good and evil.

Some philosophers, such as J.L. Mackie, question this argument, and wonder why it is not possible for God to create human beings who are completely free, and yet who *always* make the correct moral choice, instead of sometimes choosing wrongly. Could an omnipotent God not create human beings who are free, and yet who always make the morally correct choice? Supporters of the free-will defence reply that this is one of the things an omnipotent being *cannot* do (we saw in Chapter 4 that there are some logical constraints on what even an omnipotent God can do). It would be logically contradictory, Alvin Plantinga argues, for God to create beings who are really free and yet at the same time to manipulate their choices so that they always choose the right option from among the range of alternatives. It is not logically possible for God to create genuinely *free* beings who at the same time always choose the right path. The root of the contradiction involved in this scenario is that God would have to make us choose the right option in each case, yet at the same time we are supposed to be genuinely free.[4] So because God wanted to create a world in which genuinely free beings exist, he may well create a world in which evil might exist as a result of free human actions. This is because freedom is one of the highest gifts, perhaps second only to the gift of life, that God can give us. In God's eyes (and in ours), a world in which we have no free will would not be as good as a world in which we have free will. It would, rather, be a world of puppets and automata, and such a world, most would probably agree, would not be as desirable as a world with free beings.

The free-will defence seems to be a good response to the *logical* problem of evil because it would show that the existence of an all-good God would be compatible with the existence of evil, once human free will is factored into the argument. It would also be an effective response to the *evidential* problem of evil if the evil being discussed is as a result of free human actions, that is, moral evil. If we are talking about moral evil, then the free-will response shows that an all-powerful, all-good God might still create a world in which (moral) evil is possible. This is because creating human beings with free will is better than creating human beings without free will, and better than not creating human beings at all. Yet the free-will defence does not seem to be quite as good a response to the existence of natural evil. Why do we have a world which has earthquakes, natural disasters and disease in it? This is why Rowe and others focus more on natural evil than on moral evil in their arguments. What is the response of the theistic philosopher to the problem of natural evil?

EXPLAINING EVIL WITHIN THEISM

A different response to the problem is to argue that we already have good evidence that God exists independently of the problem of evil – by means of the arguments discussed in Chapters 2 and 3 – and, given this, we can then conclude that, although evil is undoubtedly a difficulty that requires our attention, it must be explained *within* theism. The argument is structured like this: 1) it is reasonable to believe in God on the evidence of natural theology; 2) evil exists in the world; 3) therefore, God must have some reason for evil. To put this argument in the context of Rowe's statement of the evidential problem, the theist might say that when one looks at the example of the fawn in the forest, one must take into account, not only the apparently pointless suffering of the fawn, but also the question of where the universe came from, in addition to questions concerning the origins and purpose of human life, the moral order, and so forth. In short, one must make an assessment of the *total* evidence relevant to the question of God's existence, not just an assessment of some of the evidence. And the theist will argue that when we take all of the evidence into account, the claim that apparently pointless evils makes it likely that there is no God becomes much less plausible than it originally appeared. For even if (let us say) we now have evil on one side of the scales against the existence of God, we also have evidence concerning the cause and purpose of the universe counting in favour of the existence of God on the other side. Even if we count evil as negative evidence against the existence of God, the balance of evidence, the theist claims, still favours theism.

In this way, theism is presented as the best explanation for the problem of evil, given that it is a reasonably plausible explanation about the origin and nature of the universe, of course. The argument does not say that, because we need to explain the existence of evil in the world, we will introduce the existence of God; after all the existence of evil was supposed to be an argument against God's existence. The argument says, rather, that given the plausibility of natural theology, theism is the only worldview within which the fact of evil has any possibility of making sense. And this, therefore, would be yet another piece of evidence in favour of theism as the best explanation. C.S. Lewis weighed in on this matter by saying that if evil counts negatively against God, might not goodness count positively in favour of God?[5] And there is more goodness in the world than there is evil. This fact would have to be factored into the weighing of the total evidence when one is judging the rationality of theism vs. the rationality of atheism. Of course, it is true that if an all-good God exists, then we would expect to find plenty of goodness in the world (but we would not expect to find evil; that is the motivation behind the problem being considered in this chapter). But Lewis's point is that we do find goodness – lots of it – and this should surely count as confirming evidence, if we want to take into account all of the available evidence, and not just the negative evidence relating to the question of whether God exists.

It has also been argued that defending atheism by appealing to the problem of evil does not help us explain or deal with the *fact* of evil. It seems to make the existence of evil even more pointless, because at least on the theistic view we have the hope and expectation that evil ultimately has a purpose, even if we cannot discern what that purpose is in this life. And if there really is an eternal paradise awaiting us in the next life, then perhaps evil will not look quite so bad from that vantage point. But on the naturalistic view, there is a sense in which everything – not just evil events – can seem pointless, since the universe and our place in it are simply accidental occurrences, and are part of no larger purpose or plan. In fact, it is difficult to see how atheists could even describe an event or happening as *evil*, given their worldview, because to describe an event as 'evil' is to suggest that it is not the way it *ought* to be. But to invoke the concept of 'the way things ought to be' in the universe is implicitly to suggest that there is a designer of the universe who should have created it in one way rather than another.

AUGUSTINIAN AND IRENAEAN THEODICIES

In order to try to provide a response to various versions of the problem of evil, theistic philosophers have sometimes proposed what are called theodicies. To propose a theodicy is to attempt to go beyond the free-will defence. Whereas the free-will defence simply says that God has a reason for (moral) evil, but does not make any attempt to speculate about what this reason is, theodicy aims to go a step further and to offer an explanation for why God allows evil. Not all theistic philosophers agree that theodicy is a worthwhile or necessary enterprise. Some theists, as I mentioned earlier, believe that the most that can be said is that we have good reason to believe there is a God, and so there must be some good reason for evil, but we cannot work out what this reason is. Some say that there is not even much point in speculating about what the reason might be, because there is such a disparity between our mind and God's mind, among other things, that such speculation would be of little use. However, other philosophers, such as Augustine and St Irenaeus (c. 141–c. 202), and more recently, C.S. Lewis, Richard Swinburne and John Hick, have tried to go further than saying that the existence of evil does not necessarily make the existence of God unlikely. They have all proposed interesting explanations for why evil exists – both natural and moral evil. Let us consider a few of these theodicies.

We turn first to a brief overview of Augustine's view.[6] Augustine approaches the task of theodicy in the way most theodicists do – he wants to explain the existence of evil without making God *directly* responsible for it. Otherwise, we have not really addressed the question of why evil exists, and have not got God off the hook. When the problem is stated this way, one can see that it is a thorny problem indeed. Augustine argues that everything that God creates is good, and so, if evil occurs, it must be explained as a *privation* or deficiency in something that was originally good. (He therefore rejected the Manichaean view that evil exists as an independent reality.) Evil does not exist as a positive force or a positive entity in itself, according to Augustine. It is, rather, a deficiency in a good thing, a bad development that creeps into something that was originally good. In this way, Augustine argues that God only creates things that are good in themselves, but because the world ended up in a fallen state, some of the things that were originally good have been subject to corruption. And this corruption is the cause of evil in our world.

Augustine accepts the doctrine of the Fall of man from an original ideal state, and the doctrine of original sin, and also links them to the notion of free will. The Fall of man occurred because of human free will turning away from God, which is also an instance of evil as privation, because it involves a deficiency in something that was originally good. He argues that the notion of free will can become the basis for an explanation for all kinds of evil, both natural and moral. It explains moral evil, because human beings are free and sometimes choose the bad, as we have seen. But it explains natural evil too, because he argues that natural evil is the work of fallen angels who are free beings, such as the devil and other evil spirits. These are beings who have continued their rebellion against God even in the afterlife. (More recently, Alvin Plantinga has offered a similar kind of argument and also links it to the free-will defence.)[7] Augustine also believes that some natural evil is God's punishment for sin.

Augustine's views have generated much discussion in the contemporary literature among religious philosophers. Philosophers have grappled with the question of whether human beings might have some freedom beyond death to act in immoral ways, and in ways that could affect us here on earth. Most no longer think this is plausible, mainly because, leaving all theological considerations aside, there seems little independent philosophical evidence to support this claim, and many reject it as implausible in the twenty-first century. John Hick, as we will see in a moment, rejects Augustine's doctrine of the Fall, and denies that human beings were originally perfect. Some atheists would also ask why God would have allowed us to *fall* from our originally perfect state into an evil world. Would God still not be responsible for setting things up this way in the first place?

Many also find the view that evil is punishment for sin implausible. This view has been a popular theory in the history of western theology (it is expressed, for instance, by Job's friends in the Old Testament Book of Job, as a reason for Job's suffering, an explanation that Job himself rejects). But it is probably a minority view today, in part because there seem to be so many obvious cases of people suffering that have nothing to do with sin. This is especially true of evil events that occur on a large scale, thus affecting a great range of people, such as the recent tsunami in Asia. If a whole village is wiped out by a flood, there will be many innocent people in the village, especially children, who are killed, as well as those who have led sinful lives. Nevertheless, some contemporary philosophers, including William Alston, have defended this view on the grounds that we do not really know what sins people may have committed, and that evil may sometimes be a punishment for sin, but not always. Alston believes that we could be mistaken about some of our moral beliefs, for example, no matter how sincerely we hold them. He also thinks that God may have some reason for horrendous natural evils that we cannot discern from our limited vantage point. Alston argues that our minds are so inadequate, especially when compared with God's, that it would not be reasonable for us to rule this out.[8]

Both John Hick and Richard Swinburne have made interesting attempts to offer modern theodicies. Let us look briefly at both views. Hick argues in his book *Evil and the God of Love* for his well-known 'soul-making' theodicy, or Irenaean theodicy. He has been influenced by the writings of Irenaeus, and offers his view as an alternative to Augustine's. Hick adopts the free-will defence for moral evil. But he argues that the reason for natural evil is that God has created a world in which our purpose is to become morally and spiritually mature. For that reason, the world is full of spiritual and moral challenges, and natural evil plays a key role in these challenges. 'A world without problems, difficulties, perils, and hardships would be morally static', Hick argues. 'For moral and spiritual growth comes through response to challenges; and in a paradise there would be no challenges.'[9] This is also why God does not make his existence absolutely obvious to us, according to Hick; there is an 'epistemic distance' between us and God, because only in this way can human beings come to know and love God freely. To achieve moral goodness in this way, Hick argues, is more valuable than to have been simply created with a morally perfect nature by God. As he puts it, 'A moral goodness which exists as the agent's initial given nature, without ever having been chosen by him in the face of temptations to the contrary, is intrinsically less valuable than a moral goodness which has been built up through the agent's own responsible choices through time in the face of alternative possibilities.'[10] In the end, according to Hick, everyone is saved, because this is part of God's plan: 'Only if [salvation] includes the entire human race can it justify the sins and sufferings of the entire human race throughout all history.'[11] However, Hick realizes that many people do not appear to be in a state of moral or spiritual health when leaving this present life, so he is forced to speculate that perhaps the soul-making process continues after death, and he even suggests that people may be reincarnated in future lives so that 'soul-making' can continue, and be completed.

This view has been criticized for being quite speculative, with very little, if any, evidence to support it. In addition, there appears to be too much evil used by God in the attempt to develop our moral character. The means seem excessive for the ends. Hick does not seem to give sufficient weight to the countless cases where evil appears to destroy people, and the cases where it clearly corrupts, and certainly does not reform. In general, certain kinds of evil seem to corrupt more than they reform. Perhaps on his view we might have to look upon certain evils as goods, because they exist in order to bring about a greater good. For instance, one could use his approach to argue that an increase in crime in a city (say of muggings) could be a positive development, because it provides all of those who are affected by the crime – both the victims and perpetrators – an opportunity to build character, the former by making them stronger (through the challenge of dealing with crime), and the latter by making them repent (which many will do eventually). In this way, many people affected by the increase in crime come closer to God in the soul-making process, develop their moral characters over time, and gradually mature into a state of grace, becoming ready for salvation.

An advantage of Hick's view is that it would explain natural evil as well as moral evil. He argues that the natural world operates according to physical laws, and these physical laws must hold consistently if we are to live in a stable universe. A stable universe is one in which much of benefit would accrue to us: for example, because the laws of physics always behave consistently we can build cars, computers and cure disease. But stability comes at a price, which is that sometimes natural evil occurs; for example, a wheel falls off a car, the car crashes and the driver is killed. As C.S. Lewis also argued: 'If fire comforts that body at a certain distance, it will destroy it when the distance is reduced . . .'[12] The point is that the stability brought about by having our universe uniformly obey natural laws makes life as we know it possible, with all its problems, but also with all its virtues.

Richard Swinburne has developed a similar argument.[13] He believes we do not simply have to rely on the above-mentioned approach of counter-balancing evidence against evil which would render the existence of God more probable than not. Swinburne offers a detailed argument that the major evils on earth, both those involving humans and those involving animals, contribute to goods in the sense that the goods could not be realized without the actual or possible occurrence of the evils. His argument is a very sophisticated version of the view that some evil is (logically) necessary for good to occur, an argument that was also expressed by Thomas Aquinas. Swinburne holds that if, for example, we are to improve our knowledge of the evil that will result from our free actions, the laws of nature must operate with consistency and regularity; yet a consequence would be that there is evil and suffering in the world. This is why God does not miraculously intervene any time the naturally operating laws of the universe are about to cause human suffering. While acknowledging that this approach is unfashionable today, Swinburne develops an intriguing argument that if God wants to create creatures sensitive to all that is good, God will allow them to have desires that are often permanently frustrated. This logically requires temporary evils along the way. A world without these evils, Swinburne argues, would not be as good as a world with them. He tries to defend both natural and moral evil in this way. Swinburne believes that this line of reasoning shows that it is very plausible to hold that an all-good God could have a *sufficient* (justifiable) reason for allowing evil. He points out that one of the reasons why people find it difficult to believe that we can make progress in theodicy today is that we have a very narrow conception of good and evil, seeing the only goods as being sensory pleasures and the only evils as sensory pains. And an all-good, all-powerful God should be able to ensure the pleasures without the pains. But this conception of good and evil is completely inadequate for human beings. Indeed, as the Greek philosophers (especially Plato and Aristotle) famously and convincingly argued, this conception is not worthy of human beings, and fails to take into account our higher qualities and faculties. So if we define the good more broadly to include the moral virtues, the development of moral character, the ability to show compassion and to seek justice, Swinburne believes that a theodicy along the lines he has suggested becomes much more plausible.

The main question that arises when evaluating these interesting attempts at modern theodicy is to ask if God could have built a natural world which mostly followed the laws of physics but which did *not* contain natural evils? Why, after all, when you are creating a world should you allow earthquakes to occur? As H.J. McCloskey has said, why not create a set of physical laws that allow us to have all or most of the good things and none of the bad effects?[14] Or perhaps a world where, when natural evil is about to occur, God directly intervenes and prevents it. For example, if a flood is about to wash away a bridge, why doesn't God intervene directly and prevent the bridge from collapsing? One obvious answer is that in many cases this might interfere with free will. This would be true if the engineers who built the bridge had been deliberately negligent. In this case, the evil would be a result of free will, not natural causes (indeed there may be a certain blurring of the lines between natural and moral evil in some cases, if, for example, one gets an illness due to irresponsible behaviour, or if we allow many to die of famine when we could have prevented it). But this answer will obviously not cover all cases of natural evil. Hick and Swinburne have argued that, even if God could have created a world where natural evil did not happen, it would not be a good thing for God to create this kind of paradise on earth. In general, these philosophers do not want to minimize cases of natural evil, but only to argue that they are not sufficient to make either atheism rational or theism irrational.

CHAPTER 6

RELIGIOUS EXPERIENCE AND GOD

The argument for the existence of God based on religious experience has received a great deal of attention from philosophers in recent decades. This argument is different in emphasis from the arguments we have considered previously, because it links the rationality of believing in God with the personal experiences of the individual in a quite direct way. It is easy to see why an argument of this form might have a considerable appeal to and influence upon a particular person, but why at the same time it might be difficult to convince others (who have not had a religious experience themselves) of its validity or reliability. The argument from religious experience belongs to the set of traditional arguments for the existence of God, but contemporary philosophers have proposed new versions of it which often appeal to useful concepts in other branches of philosophy, especially epistemology. In addition, in the United States in particular, there is great interest in the argument, because many religious believers claim to have had a personal religious experience, and will often offer this as a main reason for their commitment to the religious worldview. As a result, arguments for the rationality of belief in God that appeal to religious experiences are quite popular. We will look at some of these interesting arguments in this chapter, but before that we need to clarify what we mean by a 'religious experience'.

WHAT IS A RELIGIOUS EXPERIENCE?

Have you ever had a religious experience? How did you know it was a *religious* experience? Would you be able to describe it to a friend? Many people sincerely believe that they have had some kind of religious experience, and often these experiences affect their lives in a profound way. There are many accounts in history of religious experiences, such as Moses' experiences in the Old Testament, or the religious experiences of Jesus, or St Paul, or St Francis of Assisi (1181–1226), or St Teresa of Avila (1515–1582). There are the experiences of the religious mystics, such as St John of the Cross (1542–1591), or St Bernard of Clairvaux (1092–1153), which have inspired many, and generated much discussion and analysis. Of course, many people have not had a religious experience; indeed, critics are often sceptical about them, and believe that those who claim to have had them are mistaken; perhaps they are deluding themselves, or maybe in some cases have even 'created' or manufactured the experience. Some critics argue that all religious experiences have their origins in the psychological vagaries and susceptibilities of a fragile human mind trying to cope with an often harsh reality. The subjective nature of religious experiences has made such experiences difficult to study and analyse from a philosophical point of view. And yet, because they play a large role in the history of religion, and because they may have some validity, religious experiences are worthy of the attention of philosophers, and may help us to shed some light on the question of the existence of God, as well as on other aspects of religious belief.

There are many different types of experiences that have been described as religious, but it is possible to identify some common features that arise in many religious experiences. An experience typically described by many ordinary religious believers as religious might involve having a sense of a transcendent dimension, beyond the natural order. This might include a sense or an experience of something greater than ourselves, or it could be more specific to include a sense of a greater *being* than ourselves. This could be God himself, or it could be an experience of a being related to God, such as the Virgin Mary, or in the eastern religions it might be an experience of Ultimate Reality, such as the 'Oneness' of Hinduism. Here, for example, is John of the Cross describing his religious experience: 'Oh, you, then, delicate touch, the Word, the Son of God, through the delicacy of your divine being, you subtly penetrate the substance of my soul, and, lightly touching it all, absorb it entirely in yourself in Divine modes of delights and sweetnesses unheard of in the land of Canaan . . . How do you, the Word, the Son of God, touch mildly and gently, since you are so awesome and mighty?'[1]

St Teresa of Avila describes her experience in a quite different way:

> I was at prayer on a festival of the glorious Saint Peter when I saw Christ at my side – or, to put it better, I was conscious of Him, for neither with the eyes of my body nor with those of the soul did I see anything. I thought he was quite close to me and I saw that it was He Who, as I thought, was speaking to me. Being completely ignorant that visions of this kind could occur, I was at first very much afraid, and did nothing but weep, though, as soon as He addressed a single word to me to reassure me, I became quiet again, as I had been before, and was quite free from fear. All this time Jesus Christ seemed to be beside me, but, as this was not an imaginary vision, I could not discern in what form . . .[2]

More common religious experiences might include an experience that life is a gift, that God created the universe and that God is present.

Religious emotions can be present during religious experiences, such as feelings of happiness or of hope, or, on the other hand, feelings of abandonment or sin. Religious experiences may involve sensory awareness, either of a public or private object. In the gospels, for instance, the disciples have a public religious experience of the Risen Christ. St Teresa, on the other hand, does not seem to be able to describe her experiences in sensory terms. Rudolf Otto (1869–1937) proposed that religious experiences all involve an underlying experience of what he calls the numinous; this experience has three parts (often called the *mysterium tremendum et fascinans*) – our feeling of dependence on God, our feeling of dread or awe before God, and also our reaching out to, or our longing for, the transcendent God.[3]

TWO TYPES OF ARGUMENT FROM RELIGIOUS EXPERIENCE

It is possible today to distinguish between two quite different types of argument based on religious experience. The first might be called the *traditional argument* from religious experience, and this is the one most people are probably referring to whenever they think of arguments concerning religious experiences. The general structure of this argument involves a simple premise leading to a simple conclusion.

The premise is that many people have profound religious experiences; the conclusion is that such experiences are best explained by the existence of God. The argument does not claim to *prove* that God is the cause of the experience, or to say that we can necessarily know for sure (even if we are the ones that have the experience) that God is the cause (though perhaps this possibility could not be completely ruled out in every case). The conclusion simply says that, taking everything into account, it is reasonable to conclude that God is likely the cause of many types of religious experience.

A key move in this form of the argument is that one *infers* that God must be the cause of the religious experience. One moves logically as it were from the fact that one has a profound experience of some sort, an experience one can at least attempt to describe, to the *inference* that God is most likely the cause of the experience, or the best explanation of the experience. Some philosophers, like John Hick and Richard Swinburne, go further (as we shall see later) and argue that the inference may not only be warranted for the person who has the experience. It might also be warranted for people who may not have had an experience themselves, because they could still look at the experiences of others as reported to them – say of the saints, or of Jesus, or of their own family members or friends – and conclude that God is the most likely cause of the experience. And so one might come to regard the argument from religious experience as an argument in favour of the existence of God, even though one has not had such an experience oneself. This traditional form of the argument is well established, and has enjoyed considerable support from religious philosophers. It is based on the intuitive idea that, although some claims of religious experiences are undoubtedly false, or fake, or delusional, or mistaken, *not all of them are*. There are simply too many cases of credible religious experiences in history from very intelligent, reasonable people simply to dismiss them all as mistaken. And so, given this, the traditional form of the argument has a certain intuitive plausibility.

A contemporary version of the argument from religious experience has been proposed by Anglo-American philosophers of religion, especially Alvin Plantinga and William Alston. As we have just noted, the traditional or standard argument from religious experience holds that one makes an inference *from* one's experiences *to* the existence of God. Critics of the argument typically claim that the inference is unjustified in some important sense, that people mistakenly (for a variety of reasons) believe that their experiences are 'religious', when they really are not. It is precisely at the point of the inference, or the interpretation of the experience, that critics attack the argument. However, Plantinga and Alston believe that it is possible to sidestep this typical atheistic criticism of the argument.

They argue that, in fact, there is *no* inference involved in many cases of religious experience, that one is somehow *directly aware* of God's presence in the experience. And they believe that this version of the argument – let us call it the contemporary version – escapes standard criticisms precisely because there is no inference involved. This would be a strong argument for the rationality of belief in God, they hold, for a person who has a religious experience, and, indirectly at least, it could also be used as a more general argument for the rationality of belief in God, even for those who have not had a religious experience. Let us concentrate on this new argument based on religious experience since it has received a lot of attention. We will also refer to the traditional version by way of comparison and contrast.

THE CONTEMPORARY ARGUMENT: REFORMED EPISTEMOLOGY

The contemporary argument from religious experience has been influenced by a distinctive theological outlook which in the past has often downplayed the rationality of religious belief, and held that religious belief is more a matter of faith than reason.[4] Plantinga and Alston do not go quite this far, but they do hold that religious beliefs do not need to be justified by appeal to natural theology. Their new approach has become known as 'reformed epistemology', after the reformed tradition in theology inspired by John Calvin (1509–1564). Calvin believed that God has planted in every human being a disposition to believe in God, and that it is up to us to awaken this disposition. This view has influenced both Plantinga and Alston. There is some debate within reformed epistemology as to whether this new approach is trying to justify religious belief *philosophically*. Plantinga, in particular, has often been rather coy about claiming this, and sometimes suggests that he is simply trying to show how belief in God can be rational for a *particular* religious believer on the basis of that believer's religious experiences. He has also indicated, however, that if one could show in general that belief in God is rational for a particular religious believer on the basis of that believer's experiences, this would be a kind of indirect way of justifying religious belief philosophically. Plantinga's approach, as we shall see, also includes a critique of the traditional atheistic approach to the existence of God, and, because of this, we can also see it as an attempt to support religious belief philosophically. He tries to remove as illegitimate a certain kind of objection to religious beliefs that is based on demanding 'objective evidence' for those beliefs. He calls this the 'evidentialist objection', and tries to show that it is misplaced.

Plantinga's approach begins with a critique of the traditional epistemological theory known as 'classical foundationalism'.[5] Classical foundationalism is a fairly common-sense theory of knowledge, and some version of it constituted the main approach to epistemology in the history of philosophy. A version of it was held by both Descartes and Locke, among many other distinguished philosophers. But in the twentieth century it has come under attack, and some, including the reformed epistemologists, believe that this attack can assist religious belief. Classical foundationalism was based on the view that there are two types of beliefs, basic beliefs and inferred beliefs. Basic beliefs are obvious, ordinary, everyday common-sense types of belief, and are justified beliefs simply in virtue of being basic. Examples of these beliefs would include beliefs such as 'I am sitting at my desk now reading a book', 'I had a big breakfast this morning', '2 + 2 = 4', 'I have toothache', and so on; in short, beliefs that are, as Plantinga puts it, 'self-evident, evident to the senses, or incorrigible'.[6] These beliefs are basic because they are *not* inferred from any other beliefs. The second type of beliefs – inferred beliefs – *are* inferred on the basis of other beliefs, namely the basic ones. For example, my belief that my car needs new wiper blades is an inferred belief, my belief that Plato was a great philosopher is an inferred belief, and so on. My belief that my car needs new wiper blades is inferred from other beliefs that I also hold: for instance, my belief that the windshield is constantly dirty, that the blades do not clean the glass when it is raining, and so on. Some of these latter beliefs may also be inferred, but the chain of inferences always comes back in the end to some set of basic beliefs. Indeed, according to the classical foundationalists, all of our inferred beliefs are eventually traceable back to dependence upon some set of basic beliefs. Basic beliefs include beliefs that would fall under the general categories of ordinary perceptual and observational beliefs, memory beliefs, beliefs arrived at by introspection, and so on.

According to this epistemological approach, which many would regard as a reasonable, common-sense approach, belief in God would be an inferred belief, not a basic belief. This is illustrated by examining the various arguments we have already considered in this book. For instance, in the cosmological argument, belief in God is inferred from other beliefs we have about the world, and these beliefs are traceable to a set of basic beliefs. So, as we saw with these types of arguments, the debate in philosophy of religion is not at all about the basic beliefs, it is about whether the inference to the existence of God – the chain of inferences in fact – is justified. The enterprise of natural theology is, therefore, based on a fairly straightforward foundationalist epistemology.

Plantinga's argument is quite bold. He argues that belief in God may not be an inferred belief for a wide range of people, but may, in fact, be a basic belief. This is not to deny that for some it might be an inferred belief – if they believed on the basis of the cosmological argument, for instance – but for those who believe on the basis of their own religious experiences, belief in God is a basic belief, just like beliefs based on perception, observation, memory, and so on. In a sense, Plantinga is not perhaps attacking classical foundationalism as such; rather, he is arguing that there is a tacit *criterion* underlying classical foundationalism, a criterion for deciding what would count as a basic belief. He wants to *broaden* the criterion to allow belief in God based on religious experiences to be among the foundational, or basic, beliefs. To justify broadening the criterion in this way would require him to do two things: 1) to provide fairly clear and detailed descriptions of religious experiences; and 2) to demonstrate in a plausible way that in these experiences belief in God is arrived at in a direct way, and is not an inferred belief. Plantinga's general approach seems to require detailed work on the description of religious experiences – what philosophers call the phenomenology of religious experiences – and it is here that Plantinga's (and Alston's) view falls short in the eyes of many.

To develop his argument, Plantinga claims that classical foundationalism is based on the criterion that 'whatever is self-evident, or evident to the senses, or incorrigible' is a basic belief. And any belief not satisfying this criterion would then be an inferred belief – belief in God, for example. According to this theory, a religious philosopher would therefore be required to justify, or to give evidence for, why they believe in God. How does Plantinga propose to undermine this approach? He does so by arguing that there is no good argument to support the foundationalist criterion for what he calls 'properly basic beliefs'. According to Plantinga, the criterion is self-referentially incoherent because *it itself* is not self-evident, or evident to the senses, or incorrigible! The criterion undermines itself because it says, on the one hand, that we should begin with beliefs that are self-evident, evident to the senses and incorrigible, but then we go on to accept the criterion itself which is none of these things.

One way to reply to this point is to argue that the foundationalist criterion is an *inferred* criterion – a generalization about self-evident or incorrigible beliefs, arrived at by examining many instances of them. In this way, the criterion is not accepted because it is a basic belief; it is accepted, rather, as an inductive inference based on a rational analysis of the reliability of basic beliefs. In short, we have found that beliefs arrived at in these ways are very reliable; we can trust them and recognize that they are true. And so we have good reason after all to hold the criterion and to use it as a way of sorting out rational beliefs from irrational beliefs (or, more accurately, beliefs that need evidential support from those that do not normally need such support). If we accept Plantinga's critique of the criterion, we run the risk of not having any way do to this. His approach may invite a kind of relativism about our beliefs because, if we reject the criterion for basic beliefs, there might not be any way to decide if a particular basic belief is rational or not, and this would lead us in the direction of irrationalism.

Some have developed this critical point to argue that Plantinga is implicitly suggesting that belief in God is actually *groundless*, that we do not need any evidence or reasons to believe in God.[7] We can believe in God on the basis of various of our own experiences and, if challenged about our belief, we can simply reply that it is a basic belief. A second criticism is that Plantinga's view appears to sanction just about any kind of belief, no matter how ridiculous or poorly supported, or even dangerous. For example, what is to prevent a person who worships the Abominable Snowman from arguing that the belief is a properly basic belief? And that because it is basic, it is therefore rational and does not require any further justification.

Plantinga rejects both of these criticisms. Like Alston, he tries to draw an analogy between ordinary perceptual experience and religious experience to illustrate his argument. He gives the example of beliefs such as 'I see a tree' or 'That person is in pain', and he argues that these beliefs are justified by my experience. I do not take the behaviour of the other person when he is in pain, for instance, as *evidence* that he is in pain. My belief that he is in pain is, therefore, properly basic. The same is generally true of beliefs about memory as well; my belief that I had breakfast this morning is a basic belief. He concludes that there is a certain condition in which I find myself, which I recognize, but that is hard to state in detail, and when I am in that condition, I know that my beliefs are properly basic.

Alston has focused in more detail on the descriptions of the religious experiences.[8] He holds that religious experiences are a type of perception, and so have the same structure as perception. There are three features of ordinary perceptual experience: the perceiver (you), the object perceived (the desk), and the phenomenon or the appearance (the appearance of the desk to you). Alston holds that we can understand a religious experience as having the same three features, with the phenomenon being the way God appears to us in the experience. Obviously, religious believers report God as appearing to them in many different ways, some vague, some more specific, some involving sensory data, some ineffable. But Alston believes that the similarities between perceptual and religious experiences can help us to understand the latter more clearly.

It might be objected that these philosophers are straining the analogy too much between perceptual experiences and religious experiences. For instance, my belief that 'that person is in pain' is surely based on my seeing them in pain, and perhaps is not, therefore, a properly basic belief, and Plantinga is simply being irresponsible in seeking to expand the class of properly basic beliefs. But without getting too far off into the debate about the respective merits of various competing theories of knowledge, one perhaps could grant to the reformed epistemologists their claim that ordinary perceptual beliefs of the kind they refer to are indeed basic beliefs, for these beliefs involve ordinary, everyday perceptual experiences, which typically involve sense experiences, such as sight, hearing and touch. But a common objection to their view is that *religious* experiences are not sufficiently similar to these perceptual experiences for the analogy to work.

An experience of God does not seem sufficiently similar to seeing a tree before me now. Yet Plantinga and Alston argue that many conditions in our experience – such as guilt, gratitude, danger, a sense of God's presence – call forth properly basic *religious* beliefs, in the same way that many conditions in our experience call forth properly basic perceptual beliefs. Plantinga suggests that in some cases a person might have the belief that 'God created this flower' or that 'God is near'. This experience leads one directly to belief in God. Belief in God is somehow directly carried in the experience. This belief is not based on other beliefs, and is therefore a basic belief. But, again, we might wonder what is to prevent a person from justifying any belief whatsoever using this approach – say that one claims one has an experience of God where God has told one to live in an underground shelter for the rest of one's life? If challenged about this belief, what is to prevent a person from claiming that it is a properly basic belief, based on a personal religious experience, and further that it is rational, and not open to an evidentialist-type challenge?

In reply to this kind of objection, Plantinga thinks it is obvious that some beliefs are not justified; he gives examples of beliefs about the Great Pumpkin (from the Peanuts comic strip), or about Voodoo, or astrology. Plantinga would say that these beliefs are not called forth in the right conditions. We would discover, for example, when investigating the belief about the underground shelter that the person was not quite rational, and that his beliefs were not connected to his experiences, or that he was psychologically troubled, or something like that. So the right conditions for this person to hold the basic beliefs which he claims to hold do not obtain. Plantinga argues that the proper way to work out whether a belief is a justified basic belief is through *induction*. What we must do, he says, is to 'assemble examples of beliefs and the conditions in which those properly basic beliefs are called forth such that the former are obviously properly basic in the latter'.[9] For perceptual beliefs, an example might be 'I see a tree before me'; we know the conditions under which this belief would be justified even though it is a basic belief. If, for example, you were taking a particularly strong medicine that caused you to have occasional hallucinations of different types of trees, then you might not trust this perceptual belief, but otherwise you would. Plantinga and Alston argue that we know the appropriate kinds of conditions in religious communities which call forth basic religious beliefs. For example, in a Christian community people typically have religious beliefs of the sort that 'God is near' or 'God is talking to me' or 'God created this flower', and so forth. These are properly basic, and therefore justified, beliefs. Plantinga holds that many people have some kind of direct experience of God (which he does not describe fully), an experience which makes their belief in God basic, rational and justified. He is also saying that nobody has the kind of direct experience which the worshipper of the Abominable Snowman might claim to have, or if they do, then it could not be regarded as a basic belief, and would end up being open to question.

Critics, however, wish to push the point that ordinary perceptual experiences are not sufficiently similar to religious experiences to make analogies between them possible. Many people, for instance, do not have religious experiences of the sort mentioned, whereas everybody has ordinary perceptual experiences. This is surely a large part of the reason why the latter are not controversial, but the former are. Another problem with religious experiences is that some, such as Wayne Proudfoot, argue that they always possess interpretative elements which *motivate* the inference to the existence of God.[10] Therefore, the existence of God is not usually directly obvious in the experience (though this latter possibility cannot be ruled out *a priori*). This is why a description of religious experiences is an essential part of the debate. Let us take the experience that God created this flower. Many people have probably had this or a similar experience (and then they would form the belief that God exists). But one question raised by this type of experience is: was the experience that 'God created this flower' properly basic in Plantinga's sense, or do I form the belief *because* I am antecedently committed to the religious worldview? Since one might believe in God to begin with, one tends to see or interpret the world through 'religious eyes', as it were. The point here is that if one is committed to a religious worldview, then one might regard the world in a religious way, but this could not be taken as a *justification* for accepting a religious worldview (that is, for believing in God).

This brings us to the question of whether or not there is an *interpretation* involved in most religious experiences, a key question often asked of the traditional argument. I could report to you my experience of feeling that God's presence is sometimes near, an experience many readers will no doubt be familiar with. But perhaps I have this experience *because* I am a religious believer, committed to the religious world-picture, if you like (as Wittgenstein might have put it); I tend to see the world in a religious way. If this is the case, I probably could not take this experience of God's presence as a *reason* to believe in God, since I experience the world in this way only because I already believe in God. The second observation is that since I am interpreting my experiences in a certain way – under the influence of the religious world-picture to which I am committed – it is possible that there is an inference involved. The inference might be from some other actual experience I am having, say of the majesty and mystery of the universe, to a feeling of God's presence based on this experience. Does it follow from this, though, that I am not justified in believing in God on the basis of the experience?

From these observations about religious experiences, one cannot rule out the fact that God could make himself directly manifest to a person in some way through a religious experience. If God exists, it surely has to be possible that he could provide a revelation of himself in human experience in various ways, and possible for a person who has such as experience to *know* that it is God that is revealing himself. God can surely make himself known in this way. So we might conclude from this that while a particular individual might know for sure that it was God (such as Paul on the road to Damascus), others who hear of his report could not be so sure. One of the main problems facing arguments like those of Plantinga and Alston is that they lack specifics in terms of actual descriptions of religious experiences, specifics that might help us answer some of these questions. Without a detailed description, it is difficult for us to see whether or not there is an inference involved. One way round this difficulty might be if religious experiences of the non-inferred sort that Plantinga is talking about were very common in our lives. If many people could recognize the experiences Plantinga is referring to, then perhaps we could confirm his argument through our *own* experiences. But such experiences do not seem to be common, and there is a worry that those who do claim to have had them may have had them because they are antecedently committed to the religious worldview. This is where the similarity between ordinary perceptual experiences and religious experiences is most strained. After all, Plantinga is not talking about mystical experiences, let us remember, but fairly common religious experiences, so their features and descriptions should be readily recognizable to most people.

Plantinga and his followers can reply that such experiences *are* available to many people, even the sceptics, if only they would open themselves up to them. One may liken being receptive to religious experiences to being receptive to good music. One could be tone deaf to the beauties of music for many reasons: general lack of interest in music, denial of the aesthetic sensibility, bad experiences in music classes in school, distraction by other cultural factors, and so on. Similarly, one could be 'tone deaf' to the whole realm of religious experiences available in our universe, again for a variety of reasons: turned off religion as a child, general animus towards religion, suppression of religious insights, distraction by more worldly goods. Someone in this condition might not be easily capable of having a religious experience, might not recognize their possibility and value, may be completely tone deaf to them; yet, just as with music, religious experiences might still be real, valuable and an accurate reflection of a certain type of human relationship to the Ultimate Reality.

JOHN HICK ON RELIGIOUS EXPERIENCE

John Hick has also done some very interesting work in the area of religious experience.[11] Hick argues from the point of view of holding that the universe is 'religiously ambiguous'. He means by this that there isn't really enough evidence to decide one way or the other on the question of the existence of God. The evidence is pretty much 50/50; there is some evidence in favour of belief in God, but then there are other features of the universe which seem to indicate that there is no God. This was part of God's intention, according to Hick, as we noted in the previous chapter. God intentionally established an 'epistemic distance' between human beings and himself so that human beings could freely choose to accept the reality and love of him over time, rather than being coerced into believing in him immediately, or being initially created as morally perfect beings. Many natural theologians disagree with Hick about this, but he adopts this starting point to propose new thinking on several themes in theology and philosophy of religion, including the nature of religious experience, our main concern here.

Before we look at Hick's view, it is important to emphasize that he has been very influenced in his work by the epistemological theory of the German philosopher Immanuel Kant. Kant argued for a distinction between the world in itself, which he called the noumenal world, and the world as it appears to us, the phenomenal world. The phenomenal world, the world of appearances, is the only world that human beings can know. Kant advanced a highly complex, detailed and quite speculative account of how the human mind contributes to the act of knowing. It is not that the mind 'creates' the world for Kant; the world exists independently of us, but the world that we know in human knowledge is considerably *modified*, or constructed, by the human mind. Hick has developed a Kantian approach to religion. He holds that the religious experiences of those in the various religious traditions (as long as they can meet certain tests) are veridical. This means that the experiences of Christians, Muslims, Jews, Buddhists and Hindus represent the Real (the noumenal) in their own way, and the apparent differences can be traced to the social context – including membership in a major religion – that helped give rise to the experience. This social context – somewhat like Kant's appearances – helps account for the diversity of religious experiences. These experiences describe the phenomenal world, as it is experienced within a particular religion; indeed, all of the world's religions are individual, but inadequate, attempts to describe the noumenal world. This Kantian approach is a way around the problem of religious diversity, and it is more accurate, Hick believes, than concluding that all religious experiences are delusions, or that the experiences of one tradition are more accurate, or more correct, than those of other traditions. Many religious experiences have underlying similarities, he claims, and it is the historical and cultural standpoint of the believer that gives rise to the appearance of conflict between the various experiences.

Against this background, Hick argues that if a person has a religious experience it is reasonable for her to infer that God exists on the basis of the experience; in addition, philosophers in general can conclude on the basis of the number of reports of such experiences that God probably exists. He leaves open the question of whether or not *God* is actually the cause of the experience. Instead, he wants to approach the matter from the point of view of the question: would it be rational for a person to believe in the existence of God on the basis of having a religious experience? Hick will acknowledge that – from the point of view of the objective question of whether God exists or not – we do not know if God actually is the cause of the religious experience. But looking at the matter from the point of view of the person who has the religious experience, he is asking: is it rational for that person to believe in God on the basis of her experience? Secondly, would it be rational for me to believe in God on the basis of A's report of her experience? Hick's view differs from Plantinga's because Hick does not deny that there is an inference involved in a religious experience; yet he wants to focus on whether the religious believer is rational or justified in making the inference, not so much on whether the inference is actually true.

Hick has given special attention to the problem that Plantinga's view neglects: how we might judge whether a religious believer is mistaken or not in making the inference to the existence of God, to the question of whether or not the inference to the existence of God is justified. He initially argues that religious beliefs often arise out of a natural response of the human mind to its experiences. This is the same point that many religious thinkers have made, including Rudolf Otto, that human beings naturally react to life and the universe in a religious way, that the universe constantly pushes us in the direction of the transcendent. The question is: when you have a religious experience of this sort – what Nelson Pike calls an experience with subject/object structure[12] – what considerations might prompt you to believe that God is the best explanation for the experience?

Hick appeals to a principle proposed by Richard Swinburne called the 'principle of credulity'. Swinburne has argued that if a human being has a particular type of experience in normal everyday circumstances, then he should trust the experience.[13] This is what we do with ordinary perceptual experiences, and it should be the same with religious experiences, unless, as with perceptual experiences, there is some special reason not to trust the experience. Hick agrees, and proposes three types of test one can use to judge an experience. First, we should trust them if there are no countervailing considerations which would count against our experience. Second, we should trust our experience if it is *consistent* with the rest of our experiences and knowledge, and does not go against our existing body of belief. A third possible test of a religious experience, in particular, could be to look and see if it makes a difference in how one lives one's life. To illustrate with an example, suppose you had the experience of living in God's presence, an experience Hick believes is a fairly common experience. He does not believe this experience is a vague kind of experience to which some people might just happen to give a religious interpretation; he argues that such experiences are usually more specific, and may involve the feeling that someone is watching over us, say, or that God created the universe, or that life is a gift.

Suppose one had the experience of living in God's presence, or that life is a gift (which implies that there is gift-giver). The first of Hick's conditions would not be met if one had just been drinking heavily! This is because the experience might have occurred as a result of the drinking, and not because it was a genuine religious experience. And the second condition might not be met if it was revealed to us in the experience that we should do something immoral because this would not be consistent with the body of moral knowledge we have built up. If the two conditions *are* met, then Hick believes we should trust our experiences. He says, for example, that various religious experiences reported by the saints 'evoke a confirming echo in our own experience', and therefore we have some basis to trust our own experiences, because to some extent we see a reflection of what the saints mean in our own experience. This parallels Plantinga's point that religious experiences of the basic sort are quite common, and are a part of the fabric of the universe (as Otto also held).

Many philosophers think that the principle of credulity is a reasonable principle; it obviously requires, though, that we be careful to keep a critical eye out for possible countervailing considerations. Most religious believers will have no difficulty in doing this. And Hick is saying that if they have a religious experience then why can't it count as evidence for them that belief in God is rational; and not only for them, perhaps, but also for others who know them well, and trust them? Another possible test of the experience might be if we had independent confirming evidence that God probably exists, say from the other arguments of natural theology. This would mean that since we already have good reason to believe in God, we might be more inclined to take a religious experience seriously.

One other problem facing the argument from religious experience in general is the diversity of descriptions of religious experiences in different traditions. Although there are also many similarities in the descriptions, one runs into the problem that the Supreme Being one claims to have experienced is described differently in different religions. This seems to be a serious problem, because how can it be that the Supreme Being has all of these different, sometimes contradictory, properties, features and reactions? For example, a Christian might describe a personal relationship with God, whereas a Hindu might describe an experience of absorption and oneness with Ultimate Reality. One might respond to this difficulty by simply making the logical point that just because we have these different descriptions, it does not follow that all of them are wrong. Some of them might be genuine, some not. Perhaps in this overall discussion, we would need to take into account a religious worldview as a whole to help us figure out whether a *specific* experience was rational or not. We should also note that, given the subjective context of each believer, some variations in the descriptions are bound to occur, even if they are experiencing the same God, just as there are often conflicting *perceptual* descriptions of the same event.

Another response to this problem is Hick's Kantian approach. He argues that the range of religious experience, while constituting our human consciousness of a transcendent divine reality, takes on a great many forms within the different historical traditions. It is neither a pure undistorted consciousness of the divine, nor merely a human projection, but rather the range of differing ways in which the infinite divine reality has in fact been apprehended by finite and imperfect human beings in the various religions. So even though there may be conflicts in the descriptions of religious experiences, they are still accurate in an important sense, because they capture something true and real about the divine, even though we must acknowledge that they are partly distorted by the process of their cultural and social expression within a particular context (that is, within a particular religion).

Despite the attractions of Hick's view, it faces a number of problems, and from one point of view is quite radical. To accept his view would require, firstly, that one commit to an anti-realist Kantian approach to knowledge, to accept the thesis that the mind constructs reality in a way that has significant implications for all knowledge claims (not just those concerning religious belief). Many find this epistemological approach very problematic, because it seems to contradict our ordinary experience; others see its relativistic implications as dangerous (yet it has to be said that others may find its relativisitic approach appealing). Second, it has been suggested that the idea that we can only have limited knowledge of the real is itself unintelligible, because in order to draw any meaningful distinction between the phenomena and the noumena, we would have to know the noumena as well as the phenomena. Third, a consequence of Hick's view is that the main world religions would have to accept that their central doctrinal claims were not actually true, but simply 'perspectives' on the Real; these perspectives would have to be understood more in a metaphorical than in a literal way. For Christians, this would mean that they would have to give up their belief in the Incarnation, their beliefs about the nature of God, and about the way salvation can be achieved, and even about what salvation means. This is because if the Christian account of these religious phenomena is true, then other accounts in those religions that disagree with (or even contradict) the Christian account logically cannot be true. But it is just this kind of objective judgement that Hick says we cannot make. But accepting this kind of religious relativism is simply too radical for most religious believers across all traditions. And finally some have argued that Hick *assumes* an essential parity between all major world religions, something that he has not illustrated; in addition, even if he could establish this point, it would not follow from it that some religions are not in error about many things. We will have occasion to examine Hick's views on these matters more fully in our discussion of religious pluralism in the last chapter.

CHAPTER 7

RELIGION AND SCIENCE

The relationship between religion and science has become increasingly important in the modern world. This is not just because of renewed awareness of the historical conflicts between religion and science, but also, as noted in previous chapters, because various scientific disciplines are becoming increasingly relevant to the study of questions normally left to religion. Recent work in such areas as astronomy, astrophysics (the study of the physical composition of celestial bodies), evolution, genetics and neurology has begun to touch upon the ultimate questions of life in fascinating and challenging ways. The discipline of astronomy is obviously relevant for questions about the ultimate nature and purpose of the universe. The theory of evolution presents us with interesting conundrums about the origin and development of the species, and especially about the place of our own species, Homo Sapiens, in the overall scheme of things. The human genome project, and the possibility of genetic manipulation and engineering of species, only makes these questions all the more urgent. Recent work in neurology is relevant to questions about whether consciousness is essentially physical or non-physical, and this also raises questions about the existence of the soul, and about whether or not human actions are genuinely free, or causally determined. It is because of these, and other related matters, that no philosophical study of religion today can be complete without considering the relationship between religion and science.

It is probably true to say that the current popular understanding (the conventional wisdom) of the relationship between religion and science is that they have always had an uneasy relationship, and are basically in conflict with each other. This perception is partly based on the renown of various historical controversies which have tended to bring the two subjects into conflict. Examples include the Galileo affair in the seventeenth century and, in our own time, the controversy concerning creationism and evolution. This latest dispute has helped to keep the 'religion vs. science' model alive, and has shaped the way many people approach and think about the subject. But it is worth noting that religion and science got on fairly well throughout most of history, and that conflicts between them only arose occasionally. The first philosophers, the early Greek thinkers known as the pre-Socratics (7th–4th century BC), for instance, approached their study of reality from both a religious and a scientific perspective. They were interested in explaining such things as the order in the universe, the composition of matter and the basis of change. Philosophers such as Anixamander, Pythagoras, Heraclitus, Parmenides and Democritus approached these questions not just by using philosophical distinctions and categories, but also by application of the scientific method, insofar as this was possible in their day. And there is no question that the speculations and discoveries of these philosophers were quite profound.

There have been many other times in history when the religious worldview, especially the Christian worldview, has embraced science with great warmth and benefit. Richard Blackwell has pointed to the example of the synthesis between classical Aristotelian science and Christian theology produced by St Thomas Aquinas. He also notes that science has benefited greatly by deriving some of its basic concepts from religious sources. In the seventeenth century, for instance, the medieval conviction that the universe is a fundamentally rational place gave modern science its initial self-confidence, and the conservation laws in physics were originally suggested by the theological principle of the divine conservation of the same amount of matter and motion in the universe.[1]

One major Christian thinker concerned with the relationship between religion and science was St Augustine, as Blackwell notes. Augustine struggled for many years with the question of how the book of Genesis, especially the account of creation, should be interpreted. Augustine noted that both science and religion make truth claims about reality, and that sometimes these claims do not appear to agree with each other. So what is one to do when this happens? As noted in a previous chapter, Augustine was a strong supporter of the principle that 'all truth is one', that, since all truth is derived from

God, whatever is true in one discipline must logically be true in every other discipline. This leads us to realize, Augustine held, that in the end science and religion cannot be in conflict. He also accepts the view that science as a discipline can attain truth about the physical universe. It therefore follows that if a scientific truth conflicts with a biblical truth, one of them will have to be revised. He proposed that if we are certain that the scientific claim or theory is true, then the biblical claim should be revised. Although this approach has become generally accepted in many religions, it is still controversial, especially in the creationism vs. evolution debate, which we will look at in detail later.

But these reflections led Augustine to the question: what are we to do if a scientific claim conflicts with a biblical claim, but the scientific claim is less than certain? Suppose, as is often the case, that a scientific theory is proposed to explain a given phenomenon, but that the evidence for the theory is suggestive, not conclusive? In this situation, Augustine advised that our religious beliefs should be given preference over the scientific hypothesis. However, this approach can lead to a problem for the modern science/religion debate. This is because many scientists today, and indeed philosophers of science, are fond of pointing out that science rarely, if ever, achieves absolute certainty about anything. The best it can do is to propose theories (which are sometimes asserted as facts) that have been well confirmed by the latest evidence, and recommend that we accept these theories until something better comes along. But because the theories of one century are often shown to be false in a later century, this gives us inductive evidence that this will probably happen with current theories, no matter how sure we are that they are true. In short, some argue that every scientific theory will tend to be revised in the light of new evidence. This ambiguity about final scientific truth is often cited by those who question scientific theories today, such as the theory of evolution.

In the case of revising a biblical account, such as the creation story, Augustine believed that we are *not* saying that the creation story, for instance, is false. This is because, although the literal facts of the story might not be true, there is a deeper philosophical and theological point being made which is true: that God created the universe and all of the species, according to a particular plan, and that human beings are the highest form of species. Thus, the actual story of how God created the universe and life is revisable, according to

Augustine, but the deeper point that God created the universe and life is *not* revisable. He thought that religious believers run the risk, if they are not flexible on biblical interpretation, of being proved wrong by science. This, as Blackwell points out, is exactly what happened in the case of Galileo.

THE GALILEO AFFAIR

The potential for conflict between religion and science became obvious in the famous case which has become known as the Galileo affair. Around the year 1600, Italian astronomer Galileo Galilei became convinced that Copernicus's theory of planetary motion (which had also been proposed by some of the ancient Greek astronomers) was correct. This theory (known as the heliocentric theory) held that the earth revolved around the sun, and that the sun was the centre of the universe (and so the geocentric theory, proposed by Ptolemy in the second century, was wrong). Although heliocentrism had been around for a long time, and had generated debate among astronomers, it had little influence in the wider world. As Blackwell notes, 'the turning point came in 1610 by which time Galileo had constructed his telescope, which he then turned for the first time to the observation of the heavens'.[2] Among the observations recorded by Galileo were the mountains and valleys of the moon, four of the moons of Jupiter, sunspots and the phases of Venus. He gradually came to the view that the earth revolved around the sun, but he knew that he did not have conclusive proof. It is quite ironic that much of Galileo's evidence for the heliocentric theory turned out to be wrong (for example, he claimed that the tides were caused by the earth's motion, whereas in fact the gravitational pull of the moon and the sun causes the tides).

As everyone knows, Galileo's views led him into conflict with the authorities in the Catholic Church. As well as being an affront to common sense, the heliocentric theory seemed to contradict biblical passages, which indicated that the earth was at rest in the centre of the universe, and that the sun revolves around the earth from east to west. Passages frequently cited to criticize Galileo's views were Joshua 10. 12–14, and Psalm 19. 4–6, which suggests that the sun is in motion. As Blackwell notes, the whole discussion and subsequent controversy was made all the more intense by the fact that it took place shortly after the Reformation, when the Catholic Church was

especially sensitive, not just about questions concerning the interpretation of scripture, but also about who has the final authority on
this matter. This had been one of the major issues of contention
during the Reformation, with the Protestant reformers arguing that
individuals could interpret the Bible for themselves and did not need
the pope and the bishops as intermediaries. At the Council of Trent
in 1546, the Catholic Church declared that the pope and the bishops
had the final say in matters of faith and morals, which included questions about biblical interpretation.

This led to Galileo being put on trial by the Church in 1616. He
attempted to defend the heliocentric view by appealing to the writings of Augustine, and by appealing to the distinction between literal
and metaphorical uses of language in the Bible. Unfortunately, the
Copernican theory occupied the middle ground as Augustine had
interpreted it; it was not certain. The contemporary scientific evidence for the heliocentric theory led Cardinal Bellermine, the
Vatican cardinal dealing with the matter, to conclude that the heliocentric view was still only a theory. He urged Galileo to present
heliocentrism as a theory, not as fact. But in the meantime the
Vatican Congregation of the Holy Office officially declared that the
heliocentric view was false because it was contrary to scripture, and
Pope Paul V accepted this recommendation. (In 1992, in an address
to the Pontifical Academy of Science, Pope John Paul II admitted
that these theologians had made the error of thinking that the structure of the physical world must be decided by a literal reading of
certain scriptural passages.)

Nothing happened after this for seventeen years. Galileo went
about his work as a scientist, and kept out of harm's way. However,
in 1631 he published his famous book *Dialogue Concerning the Two
Chief World Systems*, which caused quite a stir. The book consisted
of a dialogue about the merits of the heliocentric theory vs. the
Ptolemaic theory, with the argument clearly favouring the heliocentric theory. Some of the weaker arguments were put into the mouth
of a character called Simplicius, who represented the papal view.
This led to a new trial in 1633, not about which theory was true, but
about whether or not Galileo had violated the earlier injunction
about not promoting the heliocentric theory. At this time the new
pope, Urban VIII, was under pressure from within the Vatican to
show that he was dealing effectively with dissent. This political
reality contributed to the Church taking a hard line on Galileo (an

example of how political and social matters are very often inter-twined with religious matters). He was found guilty, and sentenced to house arrest for the rest of his life.

It is worth recalling the story of the Galileo affair for a new generation of students of the philosophy of religion for several reasons. First, there are many myths about the affair, and it is always important to state the facts clearly so that one knows what actually happened. Second, the affair was very destructive of the Church's relationship with science – at least in the eyes of secularists, naturalists and those hostile to religion – and is one of those historical incidents that contributed most to the view that religion and science are inherently in conflict. The Galileo affair is most frequently cited, for instance, by those who wish to show that religion and science cannot work together. Third, it is an incident which the Catholic Church (and many other churches) learned a lot from. Thereafter, the Catholic Church was generally supportive of science, and was reluctant to provoke any more controversies with scientists or their theories. This explains why their reaction to the theory of evolution was very different. They did not want to make the same mistake twice. Fourth, the principle for dealing with apparent conflicts between science and religion, suggested by Augustine, was generally adopted by many religious believers as a good way of allowing science and religion to work together – that although the details of how God might have created the universe could be argued about, the underlying truths were what really mattered. This would become a key way of approaching science and religion in the modern era.

Unfortunately, the 'conflict model', as it is sometimes called, of the relationship between religion and science is often the first one people think of when they think about the relationship today. Indeed, while the Catholic Church was badly burned by the Galileo affair, the Protestant Churches continued to take up a generally more hostile position towards any theory that came into conflict with scripture. Because Protestant denominations placed a much higher emphasis on a literal reading of the Bible, and on the general reliability of scripture, they were very reluctant to allow any scientific theory to challenge the biblical texts. This approach also led to a general attack on philosophy and science made by some Protestant thinkers, including Martin Luther. We will come back to the Protestant critique of the theory of evolution later in this chapter.

Yet even though Christianity has often had an uneasy relationship with science, there are some thinkers who argue that it was actually the dominance of Christianity that made the rise of science possible. Stanley Jaki argues that there is a reason that science developed and flourished in the west and not the east, and that this reason was the dominance of a Christian culture.[3] According to Jaki, Christian culture held ideas that were hospitable to science: that human beings are rational creatures made in the image of God; the universe is intelligible; nature is valuable (eastern religions often had a negative view of nature); the search for truth is important; the view that all truth is one, and so forth. Jaki believes that these ideas played an important role in the development of science, especially when we take into account that for most of history the vast majority of major scientists were Christians, who saw themselves as studying God's handiwork in nature, and who frequently argued that the intricate workings of nature, which they were continually learning about, were evidence of the existence of God. This view was held by path-breaking scientists such as Kepler, Galileo, Boyle and Newton, among many others.

Jaki's argument, as well as the work and opinions of these scientists, lead us to consider the interesting relationship today between atheism and science, and to look more closely at the widely held perception that modern science is almost by definition atheistic.

ATHEISM, NATURALISM AND SCIENCE

It is quite common to confuse science and naturalism, but in order to avoid creating quite serious confusion in what is already a complex subject, it is crucial that we keep these positions clearly distinct. First, a word about secularism. In the Introduction, I defined secularism as the view that all that exists is physical in nature, consisting of some configuration of matter and energy. Since science is the means for studying the realm of the physical, then science, on this worldview, becomes the key method of trying to understand and explain all of reality. This view is also known in contemporary philosophical circles as naturalism (or less commonly as philosophical atheism). Some well-known contemporary naturalists are Francis Crick (of DNA fame), the late Carl Sagan, the late Stephen J. Gould, Steven Weinberg and Richard Dawkins.[4] I noted also that the secularist attempts to offer secularist accounts of morality and politics.

In order to clarify these views further, we might say that that part of secularism that deals with questions concerning the origin and nature of the universe (and so that would emphasize the scientific method as a way of studying these questions) is best described as naturalism, and that part that deals with morality and politics (and that would not make a significant appeal to science) is what used to be known as secular humanism. Naturalism and secular humanism have converged in the last generation or so to represent a new world-view as an alternative to the religious worldview, and I think this new view is best described by the term secularism. The development and defence of this worldview, as its various proponents work out its details and arguments on all of those topics that worldviews must be concerned with, is an ongoing project. This is why it is accurate to describe secularism as a *positive* worldview today, in the sense that it does not start by saying that there is no God; rather, it starts with positive claims about reality (such as that all of reality is physical, that we can have a secularist account of morality, and so on), and the views that there is no God, no soul and no afterlife, are conse-quences of these claims. (Since what follows deals primarily with questions of the origin and nature of the universe, rather than with questions about morality, politics and society, I will use the term naturalism rather than the term secularism for the purposes of our discussion.)

One of the main reasons for the confusion between science and naturalism is that atheistic thinkers nowadays state their views in positive terms, and this brings with it a need to *defend* one's position in a positive way. As noted in the Introduction, in the past atheism was primarily a negative worldview. But as atheism moves away from this negative way of looking at things to a more positive under-standing of itself (which requires a new name and a new identity), it will no longer be adequate from a logical point of view to try to defend positive atheistic statements by simply *attacking* arguments offered in favour of religious beliefs. So positive atheism today gets its arguments from science, perhaps especially from evolution, but also from biochemistry, genetics, astrophysics, and so forth. And this is why there is an understandable confusion between science as a dis-cipline that studies the physical realm, and naturalism, as a distinct worldview that often appeals to science.

Yet it is important to keep in mind that naturalism should not be identified with science; a naturalist usually appeals to science to defend his view, and therefore has great faith in science, but a scientist is not necessarily a naturalist, and indeed most scientists are not naturalists (which in itself is a quite significant point). Most scientists do not believe that everything that exists is physical and that science can explain everything. But because of the close alliance between naturalism and science, one can see how they often become confused, especially in the minds of the general public. But we need to realize that as soon as one goes *beyond* the scientific evidence, and makes a claim about the ultimate origin of the universe, or about the nature of human beings, or about the correct moral theory, one is crossing the line from science proper and moving into philosophy/religion, and the general area of worldviews. This is a line that scientists, *as scientists*, should not cross; nor does science as a discipline cross this line. It is only when naturalists appeal to science that there is an all too real danger of confusing the lines of demarcation that must exist between the two, and that also exist between science and *any* worldview, religious or secularist. These points obviously have implications for the contemporary controversy surrounding the topic of evolution and religion.

THE THEORY OF EVOLUTION

In order to understand further the contemporary relationship between religion and science, it is necessary to provide an overview of the theory of evolution. This is one of the most significant scientific theories of all time, and anyone who is concerned with the philosophical justification of their worldview needs to have an idea of its principal claims.[5] We can approach the theory by asking three questions: 1) what claims does the theory make?; 2) what is the evidence to support these claims?; and 3) what are the implications of these claims for religion, for ethics, and for the debate between religion and naturalism? Let us turn to the first of these questions.

The theory was first proposed by Charles Darwin, an English biologist, in his book *The Origin of Species* (first published in 1859). The research which led to the book was gathered on several voyages Darwin made to various parts of the world over a five-year period on the HMS *Beagle*, including a visit to the Galapagos Islands in 1835 (islands six hundred miles off the coast of Ecuador). The book was intended to provide an account of how all the various species we see in nature, including human beings, animals, insects, even plants, came to be. Darwin was not so much interested in what we have called the ultimate question of how they came to be, but in the more localized question of how they came to exist in nature when they did, how they came to have the physical characteristics and structure they have (though it would not turn out to be easy to separate this localized question from the ultimate question, as we will see). Before Darwin, there was no accepted answer for these questions, and many scientists believed that the species were created just as they are by God, a view that was consistent with the Bible and with Aristotle's physics. Darwin's research led him to doubt this view, and to propose a new one, which came to be known as the theory of evolution.

Perhaps the best way to approach the main claims of Darwin's theory is to work through an example, as a way of illustrating the main theoretical concepts of the theory. We can fill in other important details along the way. Let us take the example of a species of insect, the greenfly. (A species is usually defined as a group that interbreeds among itself, but that does not breed with any other group, so a species is a group that is 'reproductively isolated'.) The habitat of the greenfly exhibits a feature that many habitats, upon careful inspection, also feature: it looks perfectly designed for a greenfly to live and flourish in. We saw in Chapter 2, in our discussion of the design argument, that Paley was much taken with this point about nature. Darwin proposed, however, that the suitability of habitats for the species that live in them is not evidence of design in nature, but could in fact be explained in naturalistic ways, by appealing to the processes of natural selection, adaptation of the species, survival of the fittest, and so on.

The basic idea is that (to continue with the greenfly example) millions of years ago there were many different *types* of what we now call the greenfly, and they had different characteristics than today's greenfly. (They were not all coloured green for example.) They may also have had other variations, such as slightly different body structures, different wing spans, and so on. The theory of evolution says that over millions of years those greenflies that had an advantage over other types of flies in the same general class – who were the fittest – survived, and those who did not have this advantage did not survive. For example, the colour of the greenflies might in this specific case have given some types of greenfly a distinct advantage in the battle for survival. Flies coloured green would be better camouflaged in the green foliage, so predators hunted the black, red and yellow flies that were easier to see. Perhaps those with bigger wings were able to escape more easily from predators than those with smaller wings. A host of other factors were involved too, of course, but the idea is that eventually after millions of years there were only *green*flies left, with just the right body structure, wing span and colour, to survive in that particular habitat. This is because the greenflies interbred, and also because parents tend to pass on to their young their bodily characteristics. So eventually we ended up with *green*flies predominating and, even later, *only* with *green*flies.

Darwin did not claim to know how a particular species got its particular features; why, for instance, a particular species of greenfly was black or green or blue, and had wings of such and such a size. These features occur by means of what we now describe as random mutations (changes in DNA structure) in the genes of the species; these can be brought about by any number of factors, including the genetic structure of the parents, and the environment in which the species live. But all that matters for his theory is that these factors do affect species structure, that they are passed on to the offspring, and that they affect the struggle for survival in nature. This whole process is called natural selection – the idea that the process of evolution favours those life-forms and subspecies best able to cope with their particular environments. Those who are the 'fittest' survive best, but note that 'fittest' does not necessarily mean the healthiest or the strongest; it only means that a particular species has a feature that enables it to survive better than other similar species in the same environment. So although it looks like the greenfly and its habitat were perfectly designed for each other, they were not; it just evolved that way over time. Darwin argued that this kind of story could be told for all of the species in existence. It could also explain why many other species became extinct: because (like the yellow and black flies) they were not able to survive in the particular environment they found themselves in. The same story, he argued, can be told about human beings. Just like other species, our species of Homo Sapiens survived because our particular characteristics enabled us to survive in our environment. This overview of the process of natural selection leads to the concepts of microevolution and macroevolution, and to the question of how life began in the first place.

Up till now we have been discussing microevolution, or evolution within a species, such as the greenfly. However, there are different varieties of species that are similar to each other: for example, different varieties of elephants, dogs and beetles. Scientists often call a group of species that are more closely related to each other than they are to other species (such as different varieties of chimpanzee), a genus. When we think about this matter, it brings us to the question of macroevolution, the question of whether different species *within the same genus* are genetically related as well. If the greenfly evolved over time in the way we described, and all greenfly within one distinct species are genetically related, two questions arise. Is it the case that *different* species within the genus of greenfly are genetically related? Further, is it the case that widely different species (in different genera), such as human beings and chimps, might be genetically related?

Darwin went on to propose an answer to the question of how we get substantially different species in the first place, such as plants, elephants, chimps and human beings. This led him to the thesis known as macroevolution. Darwin came to the view that *all* species were genetically related, and the theory of evolution claims that all present species evolved from common ancestors, right back to the very first life forms, which some speculate were one-celled organisms that appeared about four billion years ago. Gradually more complex life forms developed, life forms that are genetically related to the more simple life forms. This is a key claim of the theory of evolution, and the one that has often generated controversy. The theory holds that all life forms, including all plant and animal species, are *genetically related* to each other.

What this means in practice is that at some point in the past, to take Homo Sapiens as an example, human beings and gorillas had a common ancestor (3–5 million years ago). Gradually two distinct lines of species split off from this common ancestor, one of which was Homo Sapiens (originating about 2 million years ago). A diagram of the history of this whole process is called the tree of life. It begins with one single-celled life form according to most evolutionary biologists (but some say it could have begun in different places with several different initial life forms). For the first two billion years, life existed only in microbial, single-celled organisms; but gradually over the next billion years, more complex species began to evolve, and in the last half-billion years many of our most complex species began to appear, of which the present species are descendants. Millions of species became extinct along the way. As to the final question of how the first life-form (or life-forms) got here,

Darwin, and indeed the official theory of evolution, gives no answer. The theory of evolution tries to explain the process of change that occurs when we have life-forms and an environment, and what happens is what Darwin proposed in the theory of evolution.

THE EVIDENCE FOR EVOLUTION

We must now turn to the question of the evidence for evolution, an issue which has generated much controversy in the last few decades. The stories referred to above concerning the greenfly, chimps and Homo Sapiens are mostly made-up stories to illustrate the main claims of the theory of evolution. They do not describe actual, detailed known case examples of natural selection in action that have been fully detailed by evolutionary biologists. So what is the actual evidence for the theory? There are three main types of evidence available. First, there is the fossil record. Fossils are the skeletal or trace remains of species, including plants and animals, that have been preserved in sand and mud, and other strata, sometimes for millions of years, eventually becoming sedimentary rock. Locating, studying and classifying them is a key part of evidence-gathering for paleontologists. By studying and classifying fossils, which is obviously an ongoing process, paleontologists believe that we can learn about specific species and how they lived. We can also discover closely related species that lived nearby at the same time. That way we can document the various species of elephant, for example, and also the similarities and differences between them. The close proximity of the fossils, evolutionary biologists argue, both in terms of time and in terms of location, made it reasonable to conclude that the species were *genetically* related to each other. Examples often cited include the species of whales, elephants and gorillas whose lineages have been well documented. Since Darwin's time thousands of fossils have been found and classified showing evidence of a host of species.

Critics of evolution often claim that in order to support macroevolution, many transitional species (or intermediary forms) would have to be found as well, and that not many have been found. A transitional species is a species that would be somewhere between two very different species (possessing various traits that are later separated out in the distinct species), such as the common ancestor of apes and human beings, or the common ancestor of fish and birds, and so forth. Supporters of the theory claim, however, that there are many such transitional species, and that there can be no serious debate about the evidence for macroevolution.

A second source of support for evolution comes from DNA evidence. Recent work in genetics shows that there is a 95 per cent similarity between the DNA of human beings and the DNA of chimps, and 60–70 per cent similarity between the DNA of human beings and mice (indeed some researchers have recently argued that DNA evidence shows that chimps are closer to Homo Sapiens than they are to gorillas, and so should be in the genus *Homo*, which currently contains only humans). This suggests, therefore, that such species are genetically related, based on the same principle that enables us to tell that two men are brothers, or that one man is the father of another. A third source of evidence sometimes cited is the fact that evolutionary principles can be reproduced and therefore demonstrated in a laboratory environment, where genetic mutations can be manipulated artificially, leading to the creation of altered species, and even to new species. *Mutatis mutandis*, this is supposed to mimic the way that evolution works in the natural world.

EVOLUTION, RELIGION AND CREATIONISM

One of the reasons for the controversial status of the theory of evolution among religious believers is that the theory is regarded, by both theists and atheists, as having significant implications for the debate between the two worldviews. Let us try to bring out these implications, considering the positions of Creationism and intelligent design along the way.

The first point to emphasize is that many regard the theory of evolution as challenging the literal truth of the Bible, especially the account of creation given in Genesis. The creation story in Genesis indicates that God created all of the species intact, as it were, and gives no hint that this may have been a gradual process, involving macroevolution, that took place over many billions of years. If the theory of evolution is true, then the Genesis account cannot be literally true. This is obviously one of those cases that Augustine worried about, where a scientific theory appears to clash with the Bible. His view, we recall, was that when this happens we should recognize that the Bible may not be literally true but may be using a story to make a deeper point, which is true. The deeper point that God created the universe and all life is not revisable, but our understanding of the manner in which God did this is revisable. Indeed, Augustine himself had proposed (hundreds of years before the theory of evolution) that the creation story in Genesis should probably be understood as not being literally true. But his general principle is that, when a scientific theory is established, we should reinterpret the biblical account; if not, we run the risk of short-changing science. Is there such a case here? The overwhelming majority of scientists believe that the evidence for the theory of evolution is very strong, so strong that its main claims cannot be doubted. Mainstream Catholic, Protestant and Jewish denominations have accepted this point, and have argued that there is no major incompatibility between science and the Bible, as long as we recognize that, especially in the creation narrative, the Bible is using a story to make deeper philosophical points.

Proponents of the view known as Creationism, or Creation Science, disagree. Creationism is the view that in general the Bible should be regarded as the literal word of God, and so the existence of the world, and especially of the various life-forms, came about as described in the Genesis accounts. Creationists argue that this is the most reasonable approach to biblical interpretation. And because the creation story is literally true, any scientific account of the origin of the species that differs from the biblical story, such as evolution, cannot be true. Creationists defend this view in what we might call a positive way and also in a negative way. The positive approach emphasizes the point that for Christians who regard the Bible as reliable, as the word of God, it is more reasonable to think that, in general, it should be read in a literal way because God would not reveal key features of his actions and his message in metaphors or stories, because of the danger of them being misunderstood. The creationists do not expect this argument to convince the atheists, but they do think that it is a good argument to offer to other religious believers who accept the Bible, but who favour a more metaphorical approach to the creation story. The negative approach involves leaving all issues of theological interpretation aside, and considering the theory of evolution simply as a scientific theory, and offering an appraisal of the evidence on its own merits. Creationists sometimes combine both approaches in their public discussions of this matter.

A new way of attacking the theory of evolution has recently emerged, called the theory of intelligent design, and while there are similarities between this view and Creationism, the two views should not be confused. ID theorists such as Michael Behe and William Dembski have developed an argument against the theory of evolution, and if their argument is successful it would have implications for the theism/naturalism debate.[6] They are making three general points. First, that evolutionary principles, especially the process of natural selection, cannot explain the complexity of the living cell at the molecular level. Michael Behe has proposed that the cell is 'irreducibly complex', by which he means that it needs all of its various complex parts in place at the same time in order to operate and perform its specific function. If this is true, it would raise questions for natural selection, which says that each specific part of an organism developed gradually over time, because its existence in the organism gave some selective advantage to the organism at each stage of its development. This would mean that the optic nerve, for example, evolved because it gave some selective advantage for the organism, yet the function it performed is not connected with sight, because for sight to occur we would need the eye itself, and connections to both the optic nerve and the brain, all present at the same time. So this first claim of ID theory is also at the same time a critique of the process of natural selection, but it does not necessarily deny other claims of the theory of evolution, such as that all species are genetically related (macroevolution).

The second step is then to argue that the complexity of the human cell is such that it suggests that an intelligent designer was more than likely responsible for its make-up and complexity. The third step is to argue that this is a *scientific* conclusion, not a philosophical conclusion, and so ID would be part of science, not philosophy or theology. This is one of the reasons ID has been controversial, and has generated public policy discussions in various US states (including Kansas and Ohio) about whether ID should be taught in science biology courses alongside the theory of evolution. ID theorists hold that their idea is a part of science because they argue that the claim that molecular biology shows evidence of design is an *empirical* claim, based on an investigation of living cells through various experiments in molecular biology. In short, ID theorists claim that they have examined the human cell scientifically and allowed the evidence to drive their conclusions. They sometimes compare ID to other disciplines that they believe operate in a similar way and that are generally regarded as scientific – forensics, archaeology and the search for extra-terrestrial intelligence (SETI). They often appeal to the movie *Contact* (1997), based on a novel by Carl Sagan, to emphasize that their conclusion that the human cell is designed is just as scientific as the conclusion made by the scientists in that movie that the message they received from outer space came from an intelligent mind.

The criticisms of the ID movement are many, and I will summarize them here. First, critics attack the claim that natural selection cannot explain the complexity of the cell. They frequently claim that the cell probably performed *different* functions in the past when it lacked some of the features it currently has (features that later evolved because of natural selection, and gave the cell, and the organism, some advantage it did not have previously). In short, when natural selection led to the emergence of new parts of the cell, the cell most likely took on a *new* function than the one it had before. This is how evolution works (though critics point out that specific examples to illustrate this point are pretty thin on the ground). The second and perhaps main criticism is that ID should not be regarded as science, because a scientific theory must be testable, involve measurable data, lead to predictions, and so forth. These would seem to be minimum criteria for a theory to be scientific. Yet ID theory cannot meet these criteria. It does not seem possible to come up with a way to study the nature of the designer, or to test the claim that there is a designer. The designer hypothesis seems to be outside science as science is normally understood. This is a strong criticism of ID, though it is important to note that this point is only a criticism of how ID is to be *classified*; it is not a refutation of its main claims. But one can argue that it muddies the waters too much to expand the definition of science to include ID. Why not simply argue that ID might be an argument for an intelligent designer, but not insist that it be regarded as part of science? This would be a better approach. ID theorists who work in the area of public policy reject this approach because they would like ID to be taught in high school biology courses, as a rival hypothesis to evolution. Yet it would probably be much better all round, especially for the students' education, if the theory was not presented as a rival scientific theory to evolution, but as part of a larger discussion about religion and science in a high-school course other than biology, perhaps in a social studies course. Although we are not interested in the public-policy side of the issue in this book, we should note that ID is a provocative theory, which raises interesting questions about natural selection, and about how the discipline of science is to be defined, where science ends and non-science begins, as anyone who has been intrigued by the discussion in the last few pages will no doubt agree. It is important to note also that it is incorrect and misleading to characterize ID as just another form of creationism, a common error made in the debate in the USA.

It is often in the context of this debate that some thinkers, most notably Phillip Johnson, have claimed that modern science, in refusing to consider the view that science itself might show evidence of design, is *atheistic by definition*.[7] Johnson is well known for making two broad claims in the debate on religion and evolution: 1) that the evidence for evolution is weak; and 2) that modern science is essentially atheistic or naturalistic in practice and outlook. Johnson's defence of the first claim is very interesting, and has given pause even to those who are inclined to support the theory of evolution, but he is on weaker ground with the second claim. Although he has done a great service in pointing out the atheistic tendencies of modern science, I think he oversteps the mark when he says that science is *essentially* atheistic. Science as a discipline adopts a stance towards the study of the physical realm that is called *methodological naturalism*. This approach says that when doing science, only physical, testable explanations will be considered and pursued (and so ID would be ruled out). But it does not follow from this that the *only possible explanations* for any aspect of reality are physical ones (this would be metaphysical naturalism), though it is obviously important to keep the two views distinct in one's work as a scientist, something that modern science writers, as we have seen, have not always been successful at doing. Some creationists and ID theorists, including Johnson, have mistakenly confused the view that science is committed to philosophical naturalism (only physical explanations are possible) with the view that it is committed only to methodological naturalism (*as a discipline* science deals with physical explanations by definition). It is true that some scientists are philosophical naturalists, but it is essential to appreciate that, in principle, science is generally not, and need not be, committed to any kind of naturalism. And it is probably true that in general most scientists do not believe in philosophical naturalism.

IS EVOLUTION A THREAT TO RELIGIOUS BELIEF?

There are even deeper questions, however, that the theory of evolution raises about religious belief, and that have led some thinkers to use it as a general argument in favour of naturalism. Some well-known naturalists have used scientific theories, including the theory of evolution, to defend their naturalistic approach to reality. This is part of the movement of positive atheism, as we have noted. Such thinkers include Crick, Sagan and especially Dawkins, who hold that the theory of evolution not only shows that the creation story in the Bible is false, but that in general it shows that the religious view of the world is *not true*.

This is because the theory of evolution suggests that human beings are not special in the way that most religions argue they are. Evolution shows that man is just one species among many others, and that while Homo Sapiens is the most advanced species, this is due to the blind forces of natural selection and not to design or necessity. In short, a naturalistic approach to evolution holds that human beings differ only in degree and not in kind from other life forms. This means that human beings were produced by exactly the same natural processes that produced all the other species. It is also true that the human species did not have to emerge from this process; its emergence was simply an accident of natural selection. If we replayed the tape of history, as Stephen J. Gould has put it, we would end up with different species than the ones we have now, and almost certainly there would be no species of Homo Sapiens. In addition, there is no guarantee that human beings will remain at the top of the evolutionary tree (millions of years into the future, say) because evolution is an ongoing process, and is not over yet.

Various evolutionary naturalists expand on this general way of defending atheism. They argue that evolution also shows that there is probably no soul, since human beings were produced, as were all species, from this naturalistic process. The products of this naturalistic process, such as human brains and minds, must themselves be physical in nature; and even if we grant, say, that human consciousness is non-physical, it will still have emerged from a purely physical process, and this physical process must take metaphysical priority in the order of final explanation for the existence of consciousness.

Some naturalists further extend the theory of evolution to the question of the existence of life itself, and even to the nature of the universe. They argue that the first life form most likely originated from non-living materials. This may have occurred when the right building blocks, such as methane, ammonia, hydrogen and water were present in the right environment at the right time in history, all of which would have happened by chance, of course. The experiments conducted by Stanley Miller and Harold Urey at the University of Chicago in the 1950s are often cited in this regard. Their experiments started out with only non-living materials, and attempted to produce from them *living* organisms, trying to show that this is how life could have originated on earth. They used only those ingredients they thought would have been available on earth around the time life is believed to have started. The experiment succeeded in producing amino acids, part of the building blocks of life, but only a small part, and no actual living cells. Some thought it would only be a matter of time before experiments like this did produce living things, but this has not yet happened. Fifty years later, there is little further progress on this matter; yet its supporters still point to it as likely evidence that this is how life began; others champion it as an ongoing research project that is still in its infancy.

Carl Sagan and others have defended what they call 'cosmic evolution', the basic concept of evolution applied to the universe as a whole. Sagan argues that we can describe the universe itself as evolving from the time of the Big Bang onwards in the sense that each present state of the universe is casually produced by the preceding states. This is true for all those states immediately after the Big Bang, right down to the present. Some naturalists in the grip of these theories often talk as if evolution can therefore explain all of reality. Dawkins, for example, talks as if evolution can even explain the laws of physics.

How does the theist reply to these arguments? We have already provided an overview of the theistic replies in Chapter 2, and will do no more than summarize them here. We noted that the theory of evolution presented as an argument for naturalism was a response to that version of the design argument that appealed to the notion of teleology in nature, the version which emphasizes the suitability of habitats for their species, the fact that nature seems to have been designed for a purpose. But there are other questions that the theory of evolution cannot help us with. For instance, it cannot help us with the *origin* of matter and energy. Evolution cannot help us with perhaps our two biggest questions on the subject of God's possible existence: 1) how did the universe come to be, what is its ultimate cause?; and 2) how did the design of the universe come about? ('design' here understood as the regularities present in the underlying laws of physics). As we noted, it cannot answer these questions, nor is it officially supposed to. (The official theory also cannot help us with the question of the origin of life.) The theory of evolution *logically cannot* account for the origin of the universe.

More generally, many theistic philosophers argue that because evolution cannot answer these crucial questions about the origin and nature of the universe, and so cannot answer ultimate questions about the origin of the species either, that it is no threat to religious belief. It is true that it would show that the biblical story of Genesis was not literally true, but this point was accepted by many long before the theory of evolution came along, including St Augustine. This fact, however, does not affect the deeper philosophical point behind the creation story – that God created the universe and all life for a purpose. Nor can evolution, advanced as an explanation for every fact about human beings, and so as an argument for naturalism, explain the origin of mind, or the nature of morality, both key facets of human life. So looking at the debate from the point of view of the best overall explanatory theory about the existence of the universe, the religious thinker holds that theism is still the most rational option. Philosophers who argue this way argue that evolution was directed by God, or designed by God, and that human beings are therefore at the top of the evolutionary tree by design and not by accident. In short, human beings differ in kind, and not just in degree, from other animals.

This approach leaves room for a complementary relationship between religion and science. On this view, science is not in conflict with religious belief. Science will study the realm of the physical using the methods of science in order to help us obtain as much knowledge as possible about the universe. It will adopt the approach of methodological naturalism, as mentioned above. This is fine as long as scientists *as scientists* are careful about avoiding metaphysical naturalism, which means not so much that they must not rule out supernatural explanations, but that, *as scientists*, they must be careful to avoid introducing the view that everything in the universe *must* have a scientific explanation, at least in principle. This is a mistake made by many well-known scientists in recent times: they have confused naturalism with science, which has led to this confusion creeping into popular culture, leading many to think that modern science is essentially atheistic. And so many people of good-will have become suspicious of, perhaps even hostile to, science and indeed sometimes the creationism/evolution/intelligent design debate has only added to the confusion. But as long as we keep science as a discipline distinct from metaphysical naturalism, the religious worldview can fully embrace the scientific method, and has nothing to fear from the scientific method. Theistic philosophers who support this view hold that because the religious worldview is the best overall explanatory theory of reality, that science will take its natural place within this position, and so religion and science can work together in the quest to understand reality.[8] Each scientific theory will be accepted on the basis of an assessment of the evidence for the theory, including the theory of evolution. Nothing less is required by a commitment to reason. And religious belief has nothing to fear from reason.

All of this brings us to the fascinating topic of human consciousness. Before we conclude this chapter, we need to elaborate briefly on the important issues of mind, consciousness and soul as they relate to the religion/science debate and dialogue.

MIND, SOUL AND IMMORTALITY

It is a central belief of most religions that human beings survive death in some way, and that many achieve immortality. Belief in immortality is crucial to many religions, because for human beings it is the link between this life and the next life, and also because it suggests that what one does in this life is important for what happens in the next life; it suggests, in other words, that we will be judged in the next life. This is how many religions work out their view of salvation. But although most religions have believed in immortality in some form, and indeed most people today around the world continue to believe that they will see their loved ones again in the next life, are there any philosophical reasons for believing in immortality? Leaving theological considerations aside, what has philosophy to say about immortality? And can current science help us at all with this question?

Philosophers today are interested in several issues relating to immortality. One is the question of what immortality means – that is, how are we to understand our survival after death? What would be necessary in order for it to be *me* who survives (the question of what constitutes personal identity)? A second question concerns whether it is only our soul that survives, but not the body, or the soul and the body?

Let us start with the second question, which takes us into the area of philosophy known as philosophy of mind.[9] Arguments in the philosophy of mind concerning immortality have been especially prominent in recent times, as the debate between theism and naturalism becomes a central focus. It is no accident that philosophy of mind is one of the hottest areas in philosophical research today. This is because it raises hotly disputed issues among various worldviews concerning the nature of the human mind and its activities. The central question in the philosophy of mind, the body/mind problem, is: what is the relationship between the body and the mind? By the mind is meant consciousness, thoughts, reasoning ability, logic, memories, imagination, and so on. The body refers to the physical stuff of the brain such as the cortexes, neurons, cells, membranes and dendrites. An argument for immortality based on the body/mind distinction is at least as old as Plato. Although Plato had specific arguments for immortality, his general point was that what happens at natural death is that the body dies, but the mind survives. The body is a physical object, and, like all physical objects, it is contingent, has a finite lifespan, and will eventually die and decay. But the mind is a non-physical, mental, spiritual substance, the seat of our consciousness, memories and personal identity, and it will survive the death of the body. This general approach gradually developed into a well-known argument in the history of philosophy in favour of immortality. René Descartes (1596–1650) was another famous exponent of this view, a view which became known as substance dualism.

Substance dualism is opposed to materialism, the other main position about the body/mind relation. Materialism is the view that the human mind is either completely physical, or that it depends upon the physical. Some philosophers take a strong view of materialism and argue for mind/brain *identity*. This is the view that the human mind and the human brain are the same thing, they are identical. It is not that these philosophers deny that consciousness, thoughts and logic exist; they simply deny that these features are non-physical, but are, rather, sophisticated, complex *physical* operations of the brain, and although we do not yet fully understand how they work, we will in the future through further scientific research. Other materialists take a more moderate view: they hold that the activities which we normally understand as belonging to the human mind *might* be non-physical, but even if this is the case, they are still produced by the brain, and therefore are completely dependent upon the brain. On either view, immortality could not be defended by arguing that the mind will survive the death of the body, because on mind–brain identity theory, there is nothing non-physical to survive, so when the brain dies, everything dies. Yet even on the moderate view, when the brain dies the mind will die also since it depends for its existence on the physical. There are several other positions in between materialism and substance dualism that one might take – indeed moderate materialism is one of them – but we do not need to get into the details of these positions for our discussion here. The main point to be aware of is that the dualist view generally holds that the non-physical mind can survive death in some form, and so this would be a reasonably good explanation for immortality, and the materialist side denies this.

Let us consider briefly some of the arguments offered by the dualists for the claim that the human mind can survive the death of the body, and also consider how the atheistic materialist might reply to them. The first argument offered by the dualist is the argument from properties. This argument appeals to the logical principle that if two things have different properties, then they cannot be the same thing. Descartes famously argued that this is the case with the body and the mind. The mind cannot be literally measured, weighed, or divided up, but the brain can. It makes no sense to talk about how heavy my idea of New York city is, but it does make sense to ask how heavy my frontal lobe is! This argument shows that the mind is of a different order than the brain, of a non-physical order, in fact. The materialist replies to this argument by saying that although two things may appear to be different, they might not be. They often appeal to the example of the planet Venus, which is sometimes referred to as the evening star and sometimes as the morning star, because it appears in the evening sky and the morning sky at different times of the year. People might easily think these were different stars (like the Greeks, for example, who named them Hesperus and Phosphorus) because they appear to have different properties (one rises in the morning and one in the evening) yet they are in fact the same star. Although this is not a perfect analogy, because the evening star and the morning star are at least both stars (and so there would be some basis for the possibility that they could turn out to be the same star), the materialist argues that it could be the same with the body and the mind.

Another argument appealed to by the dualist is the argument from intentionality. This argument draws attention to a very peculiar property that our mental states (our thoughts and ideas) have, a property not shared by physical objects. Let us appeal to a thought experiment to illustrate the unusual phenomenon of intentionality. Think about your home for a moment; form a picture of it in your mind. Now if I ask you: what you are thinking 'about'?, you will answer, 'I am thinking about my home'. You are not thinking 'about' the university library. The ideas and pictures in your mind are said to have intentional content, they are 'about' or 'of' something out there in the real world (in extra-mental reality, or the world outside the mind). This is true for most of our beliefs, concepts, ideas, arguments, and so forth. It is a remarkable property of the mental. The dualist claims that intentionality cannot be explained in physical terms, because it makes no sense to say that the atomic or molecular structure of a physical object (such as brain cells) could be *about* another object distinct from it. Nor does it make much sense to say that a physical object could produce a non-physical effect, which would have as one of its features the phenomenon of intentionality. The materialist would need to explain the existence of intentionality in a scientific way involving an account of the workings of the human brain. What is required is an explanation in terms of physical properties and scientific causal laws. The dualist argues that this cannot be done.

The materialist usually offers one of two arguments in reply, neither of which are very convincing, to my mind (no pun intended!). They argue, firstly, that intentionality may well have, and probably does have, a physical explanation. It is just that we have not discovered it yet. I like to call this the 'scientific-faith argument' in the philosophy of mind. It is an argument that is often appealed to by the materialist who is faced with recalcitrant features of the mind that seem to resist physical, scientific explanations. It is based on the claim that, since there have been many things in the past that we could not explain but now can explain, such as lightning, it will be the same with intentionality, and indeed with the mind more generally. The dualist does not deny that the scientific faith argument is a good argument in science (when applied to lightning) but denies that it is a good argument when applied to intentionality, or to the mind more generally. This is because intentionality, unlike lightning, is not just another physical object, and seems to have no basis in physical matter, such as atoms and causal laws. Therefore to treat it as if it were just another physical object is far-fetched. The second reply of the materialist is to suggest that intentionality might be some kind of illusion, in the sense that the 'aboutness' is actually *of the mental state*, not the object in the world (an 'aboutness' that would still have to be explained).

A third argument offered by the dualist might be called the argument from free will. Many believe this argument to be a decisive argument against any theory of materialism about the human mind. Free will may be defined as the ability of human beings to make a genuine choice between alternatives, a choice that is not determined by scientific laws operating on atomic or molecular particles or combinations of particles in the brain. Without genuine free will, morality would make no sense, since the whole enterprise depends on human beings having a genuine choice between good and bad. Similarly, moral responsibility, punishment and even democracy all depend on the prior belief that human beings have free will. The dualist argues that since human beings have free will, materialism must be false. This is a very thorny problem indeed for materialists who are faced with saying that, since all of our actions are rooted in our brains and central nervous systems, then all our 'choices' would be explicable in terms of scientific causal laws, operating on bits of matter. We would be like sophisticated robots, whose very operation is determined by causal sequences functioning according to scientific laws. In short, there is no room for free will in a naturalistic universe.

Materialists have long struggled with this notion, and are really only starting to come to terms with the problem that free will creates for their view. They realize that it is almost impossible to conceive of human life as we understand and experience it without believing in free will, and so the cost of giving it up is massive, and yet they can see no way of fitting free will into a completely physical universe. That is why they have often experimented with what are called compatibalist notions of freedom. These are based on the apparently contradictory view that although all of nature, including human beings (and the human brain), are subject to physical laws, human beings can still be free. Although these theories are interesting, it is hard to see how they could be true since there is an apparent contradiction at the heart of them; but one must resort to something like them in order to deal with this problem for materialism.

The dualist claims that because the mind is non-physical, it has a certain independence from the brain, and that it follows from this that it is possible for it to survive bodily death. Given the radical difference between the body and the mind discussed in the above arguments, the proposition is that although the mind and the brain certainly work together in this life, there is no logical objection to saying that the mind could survive the death of the body. Since the mind would also involve our consciousness, ideas, memories, and so forth, this would also be an argument that it would be *us* that survives – that our personal identity would be maintained in the afterlife. Sometimes materialists reply by invoking the 'brain injuries' argument. This is the argument that when the brain is injured, there is often a corresponding loss of mental function, and this shows that the mind is dependent on the brain for its activities. The dualist replies that this argument would show that, in this life, the brain is a *necessary* condition for mental life, but it does not show that it is a *sufficient* condition for mental life. Nor would it follow that after death the mind could not operate without the body. The arguments discussed above, the theist argues, point to the fact that the mind is more than the brain. So it could still be the case that the mind can function on its own, without needing brain events, and that this can happen in an afterlife.

Philosophers have differed over what form the afterlife might take. There have been a variety of positions on this matter, which we can only sketch here as a way of whetting the appetite of those interested in pursuing this fascinating topic further. In the west there have been two main views. One is that the mind alone is enough to guarantee one's personal identity in the afterlife; the body is not required. The second view is that the body will be resurrected, and will eventually be reunited with the non-physical mind. Some eastern religions have adhered to theories of reincarnation. Reincarnation requires a belief in dualism, because it holds that the mind survives bodily death, and is then reincarnated in another body. This process can go on over several generations, before the soul eventually escapes the cycle of birth, death and rebirth. This is what it means to achieve salvation. Eastern views of immortality have often explained the afterlife as a place where the individual consciousness is absorbed into an undifferentiated 'Oneness' (as noted in Chapter 4). We can understand this view better perhaps if we invoke the metaphor of regarding one's consciousness as being in a jar in this life, and death as an escape from the jar into an overall Oneness, which is the ultimate reality. This is in contrast to western views of immortality, which have strongly emphasized the fact that the individual retains his or her individuality in the afterlife (this is why questions of personal identity are important) and achieves a personal relationship with God.

Before concluding, we should mention other scientific evidence that might be brought to bear on the questions of the body/mind relation and of immortality, such as evidence concerning telepathy, various psychic phenomena (like extrasensory perception), near death experiences, and so on. Telepathy and ESP, for example, would be further problems for materialism in the sense that, if confirmed, these practices would seem to support the view that the mind is non-physical, since they would seem to involve mental activities that could not be easily explained in terms of physics. The phenomenon of near-death experiences and out-of-body experiences is fascinating. These are experiences reported by many people who had been close to death, but later recovered. They typically involve an experience of being outside one's body, often accompanied by sensations of being in a tunnel in the presence of a bright light, accompanied by feelings of peace, love, acceptance, and so on. There seems little doubt that such experiences occur. The question is how to explain them. If eventually supported with good evidence, dualists will claim that they support mind–body dualism, while materialists will say that they are probably caused by chemical reactions in the brain triggered by the state of being near death.

We must emphasize that the evidence for all of these human activities is not yet in, and that current evidence related to them is much disputed. Our aim here is simply to note how these apparently disparate phenomena are relevant to the body/mind discussion and related questions, including the question of immortality. It is yet another reminder that many issues we might often discuss as interesting issues in their own right often have a place in the religion/science discussion, and in the larger discussion concerning worldviews and the meaning of life.

CHAPTER 8

RELIGIOUS DIVERSITY: IS THERE A TRUE RELIGION?

The widespread diversity among the world's religions gives rise to what, in the philosophy of religion, is often called the problem of religious pluralism. The existence of widespread religious diversity throughout various cultures inevitably forces us to ask what the implications are of this diversity for the truth of religion in general. Does the fact that there are a variety of religions in the world mean that somehow any one religion is just as legitimate as any other? Or does it mean that none of them can lay claim to truth? Does the fact of religious diversity undermine our confidence in our own religion? Indeed, the presence of different views on the important questions of life has led to a relativism, even scepticism, among many in the modern era on the question of discovering truth about key matters of morality, law, politics and society. So it should not really be a surprise that this relativism and scepticism have some influence on religion as well.

One must keep before one's mind the many religions of the world when thinking about these questions. Although our focus in this book has been on Christianity, we must also think about Islam, Judaism, Hinduism, Buddhism, Taoism, Confucianism, and so forth. It is simply not possible for us to ignore other religions in today's cultural climate. Global communications and ease of travel have brought the major religions into contact with each other more than ever before in history, and this fact alone calls for us to confront the question of religious pluralism. It is more common today for people of one religion to know and indeed to work with people who are members of different religions. In general, religious believers are becoming more interested in, and respectful of, other religions. Yet there are obviously quite significant differences between religions on many matters: the nature of God or ultimate reality, the correct account of revelation and sacred texts, moral issues, and especially doctrinal issues, such as the Incarnation and the Resurrection, which Christians affirm, for instance, but which Muslims deny.

Let us not forget also that questions posed by pluralism are questions members of *all* religions must face. These are not just concerns for Christians. Followers of each religious worldview must ask critical questions not just about the truth claims of their own worldview, but also about how they regard the truth claims of *other* religions. This is a vitally important matter because, although religions do agree on some issues, they disagree about many things as well. Sometimes these disagreements can be serious, and can lead to arguments about the correct understanding of, and path to, salvation. Indeed, salvation is perhaps the key concept in the discussion about religious pluralism. The concept of salvation should be understood in a quite broad sense to refer to the correct path to eternal life and happiness (if there is one). This definition is preferable to the narrower one which might focus on how salvation was provided for in a particular religion (such as through the death and resurrection of Jesus in Christianity). Although the narrower understanding is very important, and we will come back to it again later, the broader question allows us to think about the general matter of salvation as it applies to all of the world's religions. One of the central questions that gives rise to contentious debate between religions concerns whether members of religion A believe that members of religion B can be saved, and vice versa. And what does religion C believe about members of A and B? Is there only one true religion in the sense that the path to salvation is available in only one religion, or can salvation be achieved in many different religions? Or is one prepared to respond to this problem by saying that there is no such thing as salvation? These are the questions we will explore in this chapter.[1]

Before getting into these questions, it is interesting to speculate about whether there is a place for the secularist worldview in this debate. The problem of religious pluralism has always been understood in the philosophy of religion as a problem about how to understand and respond to the fact that there are many different religions in the world, as we have seen. Yet, as I suggested in the Introduction to this book, once we come to appreciate that secularism is a major worldview in its own right in the modern world, it is sometimes appropriate to broaden our discussion of at least some religious topics to include the secularist position on these topics as well. Indeed, as I noted earlier, many issues in current philosophy of religion come down to a debate between religious and secularist views of the world. Yet it is not easy to see how the questions raised by religious pluralism could easily be broadened to include secularist perspectives as well. This is because the matter of salvation is central to the topic of religious pluralism, and the secularists hold that there is no God, no afterlife, no soul, and therefore no salvation. But suppose, in order to push this thought experiment further, that instead of appealing to salvation as the key concept raised by the debate about diversity (or instead of understanding salvation in a specifically religious way), we appeal to the concept of ultimate truth, or the correct path to happiness, or something along those lines.

So we could ask about the diversity of worldviews – now including secularism – if the secularist believes his worldview to be the ultimate truth, or provides the correct path to happiness (with whatever account of happiness secularists wish to defend). Or we might ask how a secularist would respond to the question of truth with regard to the diversity of worldviews in general (religious and secularist). This would be the equivalent of asking, of a particular religion, whether its members hold that it alone contains the ultimate truth or the true path to happiness. Although we will continue to treat the problem of religious pluralism in this chapter as a problem for religions only, it can be helpful to keep in the back of our minds how the questions in this chapter would apply to secularism. This is important because, given that secularism is a major cultural player in itself these days, especially in some countries, it is no longer appropriate to ask questions about how we should deal with the diversity of worldviews in the modern world, and not to consider secularism as one of these worldviews. Or to put the matter another way: it is no longer appropriate to restrict these questions to religious believers; we must now ask them of everyone who holds, practises or advocates a worldview.

Before going on to consider the three main responses to the problem of religious diversity, it is necessary to make a few preliminary points. First, in our reflections we need to focus clearly on the matter of the actual truth claims of our own religion. This means that one needs to think carefully about what one's religion is saying about God, about reality, about the nature of human beings, about our relationship to God, and about morality. What does your religion claim is really the case, is objectively true about these matters (and not just a matter of convention or opinion)? These kinds of claims are often called metaphysical or ontological claims by philosophers. It is because the metaphysical claims of various religions are often quite different that we can say that some religions contradict each other; for instance, Christians hold that when we die we will probably enter into a personal relationship with God immediately, whereas Hindus hold that we will be reincarnated. On the face of it, these claims cannot both be true.

Second, a member of a religion should also ask if the metaphysical claims of their religion are rational. As I have emphasized throughout this book, the rationality of one's worldview is very important. Indeed, we might think of the problem of religious pluralism in terms of three questions: 1) What metaphysical claims do I hold in my religion? 2) Are these claims rational? 3) What is my response to other religions that make *different* metaphysical claims? Do I think that these other claims are false, or that they undermine my own religious beliefs, or that all of them can somehow be true, or that none must be true?

Third, we need also to keep in mind the difference between the theoretical claims or beliefs of a religion and the practical effects of these claims in the life of a believer. The theoretical claims refer to the beliefs a religious person holds on a variety of topics (theological, doctrinal, moral, and so on); focusing on these claims gives rise to the question of the truth of these beliefs, the question of what are the right beliefs to hold. The practical effect of the beliefs in the life of the believer refers to how a religious believer actually lives out her religion in her ordinary, everyday life. This matter raises the question of *what is the correct way to live morally*, a key concern of religion in general. The distinction between the theoretical claims of a religion and the practical effect of those claims in the life of the believer is an important distinction, because sometimes while the theoretical claims can be quite diverse among different religions, the practical effects of religious claims can be quite similar, at least in some important respects. And this fact might have some significance for our understanding of, and response to, the problem of religious pluralism.

RELIGIOUS EXCLUSIVISM

The first view we will consider as a response to the problem of religious pluralism is known as religious exclusivism. This is the view that the correct path to salvation can be found in only one religion. This view is very widely held today among all religions; it was also the main approach to the question of religious pluralism throughout history. The Catholic Church, for example, teaches the doctrine of *extra ecclesiam nulla salus*, which means 'outside the church there is no salvation', and for a long time this was understood in an exclusivist way (though attitudes to this within the Catholic Church changed after Vatican II). Many Protestant denominations, mutatis mutandis, hold a similar view. The Protestant theologian Karl Barth (1886–1968) is a well-known exponent of this view.[2] Religious exclusivism is a position one can adopt whatever religion one holds; it is also probably true to say that all major religious have held some version of exclusivism, or still hold it. It is also possible to take a narrow position or a wide position on exclusivism. Those who take the narrower view would hold that membership of a particular religious denomination is required to achieve salvation, while those who subscribe to the broader view might hold that anyone who is, say, a Christian (or whatever religion we are talking about) will be saved, irrespective of their particular denominational affiliation.

Today religious exclusivists sometimes object to the term 'exclusivism' as a label for describing their position, because they argue that the term has negative connotations, conveying the idea that this view is isolationist, insular and intolerant. They object that the term 'exclusivism' is a politically correct term developed to isolate their views without actually engaging with them. Some therefore prefer to use the term 'particularism' instead (a more neutral term) and one which, in the current climate of political correctness, is more likely to get a fair hearing for this view. Religious exclusivists do hold that there can be profound truths in other religions, but their main claim is that one cannot achieve salvation if one follows the wrong religion. Just because a religion is right on some points does not mean that overall it contains the right beliefs and actions that would lead to salvation. Judging whether another religion is right on some points will depend for the exclusivist on whether it agrees with the correct religion on these points; for instance, a Muslim who subscribes to exclusivism might believe that Christianity is right in believing that God is all-powerful, but would deny that Christianity can lead to salvation.

It is evident that for religious exclusivists, missionary work is very important. This means that the religious exclusivist will take seriously and devote a lot of time and energy to the task of nurturing, explaining, defending, promoting and propagating their religion with a view to gaining converts. This is an urgent task for the church, because the salvation of people's souls is at stake. Missionary work can be carried out in a variety of ways, and could include a religion getting directly involved in politics as a way of spreading influence. Any objections to this involvement would be outweighed by the fact that people's eternal souls are at stake.

What are the arguments for exclusivism? Exclusivists have developed three main lines of argument.[3] The first is a philosophical argument. This argument has four main points. The first point is that it is reasonable to believe that God exists using the arguments of natural theology, like those we have considered in this book. This leads to the second point: since God exists, it is reasonable for us to expect a revelation from God of his plan for human beings. So we should look around in history for evidence of such revelation. The third part of the argument involves examining the various candidates in history for the true revelation, and arguing that one particular revelation (the Bible for Christians) is superior to the others. This particular argument would involve appeal to historical evidence, textual analysis, moral theology, philosophical arguments about textual interpretation, and so on. The last part of the philosophical argument involves illustrating that the correct account of revelation teaches that an exclusivist position on salvation is true – for instance, that the Bible teaches that there is only one way to salvation (and that this is captured best in one particular religion or denomination).

The second argument for exclusivism is more straightforwardly theological in character, and has probably been the main argument appealed to in the history of theology and philosophy. This view simply starts with a given revelation as true, and argues that this revelation teaches that there is only one true way to salvation. The revelation may be backed up by appeal to historical evidence and theological debate, but it is not generally part of a larger philosophical argument, such as the one considered above. In short, the scholars in each religious community have from time to time considered the question of why their revelation is better than others, but they have not generally appealed to natural theology-type arguments as part of this overall case. They have restricted themselves to an analysis of a particular revelation event, and the texts and traditions that arose out of it.

The third argument behind religious exclusivism is a logical one.[4] This argument makes the point that as a simple matter of logic not all world religions can be true. Even if there is some truth in all of them, there still remain straightforward contradictions between them, so some of these religions logically must be wrong on some matters. It could be the case that all of them are wrong, of course, but the exclusivist, because he believes that a religious view of the world is generally true, holds that it is more reasonable to think that one of them is nearer to the truth than the others (even if we acknowledge that none may have the full truth). At least we can know, the exclusivist holds, what the correct path to salvation is. The exclusivist also frequently rejects modern-day criticisms of exclusivism on the grounds that they are not based on a rational analysis of the question of which revelation is more likely to be correct, but are instead based on an unwillingness to face up to the question of, and to have a real debate about, the respective merits of different worldviews. This is because many today are intimidated by multiculturalism and political correctness into not asking hard questions about different views, and are afraid of offending others.

Despite these interesting and challenging arguments, there are significant problems facing the position of religious exclusivism. One objection many raise is that while the logic behind the exclusivist position makes sense, it is simply not possible to make an accurate, reasonable judgement as to which world religion is the true one and, therefore, as to what the correct path to salvation is. There are simply too many grey areas concerning historical evidence, the dating of texts, eyewitness accounts, claims of the miraculous, conflicts of textual interpretation and the content of religious experiences to make a judgement, and therefore the view that only one religion has the true way to salvation is not realistic. It is too much of a stretch, critics say, to believe that the outcome of such a debate would be to conclude that one particular religion provides the only true path to salvation.

A second line of argument against exclusivism is that many see no logical or theological difficulty in the view that God could have revealed himself in different ways in different religions. Perhaps God revealed himself in ways suitable to a particular culture, time and place. Exclusivists reject this because they believe that it is too vague, and because they can see no difficulty for why a powerful God could not reveal himself in substantially the same way in different cultures. Revealing himself in different ways would simply lead to confusion, and would have the effect of unnecessarily leading people astray. Besides, it is one thing for God to reveal himself in different ways, but why would God reveal different *messages* in different religions? Some might wonder how we can fault people for being sincerely believing members of the dominant religion in their culture. Some suggest that if a sincerely believing Muslim had been brought up in a different culture, say a Christian one, he would instead be a sincerely believing Christian, so how can one fault him for being a sincerely believing Muslim? Exclusivists accept this point, but they don't think it is relevant to the debate; they argue that it does not follow that because one absorbs the worldview of one's culture that that worldview is true. They also hold that one is not *totally* shaped by one's culture, but can remain independent enough to get a critical perspective on it, even though this can sometimes be difficult.

One of the strongest reasons for rejecting exclusivism, its critics hold, is that it seems quite unfair to members of the wrong religions. This is because, although it might be true that in theory one can take a critical perspective on one's religion, this is more difficult to do in practice. This fact, coupled with the fact that, for ordinary believers, comparing the different religions in terms of their truth is an impossible task, it would be very unfair of God to condemn eternally any person who failed to convert to, and to follow, the correct religion. This is sometimes couched as a *moral* objection to exclusivism – that it would be immoral of God to set things up in such an unfair way. Because it would be immoral of God to do this, this view cannot be correct, and, further, it is immoral of exclusivists to insist that it is correct. An extension of the point about unfairness is that exclusivists need to think about what would happen to people who have not followed the correct religion *because they have never heard of it*. In this case it would be through no fault of their own that they do not accept the true religion.

Some exclusivists respond to these challenging objections by holding that such people will be given another opportunity to respond to God after death. Others resort to a complicated and very contentious doctrine of God's 'middle knowledge', known as

Molinism (after the seventeenth-century Jesuit theologian Luis de Molina) to solve this problem. This view holds that in addition to God's knowledge of the past, present and future, he also has a type of knowledge called middle knowledge. God has middle knowledge if he knows what you *would* have done had you been presented with certain choices in your life, which, in fact, you were not presented with (these are called contrary to fact, or counterfactual, choices). So, on this view, God knows what you would have done *had you been* presented with the correct religious view of salvation. He knows whether you would have accepted it or not, and will grant or deny salvation accordingly. For many, this is a speculative doctrine, and also runs into the problem of the compatibility of God's knowledge of possible events and human free will, yet it is an essential doctrine for the exclusivist because it is necessary for him to have a response to the difficult problem of what happens to those who through no fault of their own have never heard the truth.

RELIGIOUS PLURALISM

Those who hold the position known as religious pluralism are often critical of exclusivism in particular, and have developed pluralism as an alternative position. Religious pluralism is the view that there are many different ways to salvation in the various world religions, and so all religions have a certain legitimacy. A strong, perhaps more extreme, advocate of this view is John Hick. As indicated in earlier chapters, Hick has been influenced by Kant's metaphysics; he believes that Kant's distinction between the phenomenon and the noumenon gives us a way to develop a plausible argument for pluralism. As noted in Chapter 5, Kant distinguished between the phenomenal world and the noumenal world, between the world as it appears to us and the world as it is itself. He claimed that we only know the phenomenal world, which, although based on the noumenal world, is modified in a significant way *in the act of the knowing*. In addition, the human mind cannot escape these modifying acts in order to know the world as it is in itself.

Hick applies these categories to the problem of religious diversity.[5] He argues, for instance, that the nature of God or Ultimate Reality is equivalent to the noumenal world. The Real or the Divine, as he sometimes refers to Ultimate Reality, is beyond human comprehension; it is in the realm of the noumenal. However, human beings reach out from their limited perspective to attempt to describe the noumenal, which they do in different ways, and these varying descriptions give rise to the different world religions. Each of the different religions represents different phenomenal perspectives on the noumenal. It follows then, according to Hick, that none of them has the whole truth about the Real, for this is impossible. But it also follows that each of them has a legitimate perspective on the Real, and so no one religion can claim to be more true than another, or to represent the only true path to salvation. This is true, Hick argues, even when the religions contradict each other, a point that exclusivists argued logically shows that not all religions can be true. Hick deals with the problem of contradiction by saying that each religion is so far removed from a correct description of the Real, that although different claims look like they are contradicting each other – for example eastern and western views of immortality – they are best described as 'distortions' because they fall so far short of the truth of the matter, a truth beyond human comprehension.

To illustrate how this might work, Hick, and many other pluralists, appeal to the story of the blind men and the elephant. A group of blind men have to describe an elephant, an animal they have never encountered before. But they each approach him from different sides. So the first feels a leg and reports that he is a great living pillar; another feels the trunk and reports that he is a great snake; yet another feels a tusk and reports that he is like a sharp plough-share; and so on. These descriptions are all correct in their way, but because of the respective limited approaches of each blind man before the majesty of the elephant, each description falls far short of the correct description, the one that would capture what the elephant is really like in himself. So it is with the various religions (represented in the story by the blind men), and the Real (represented by the elephant). Just as two descriptions from the blind men appear to contradict each other, but are actually both correct in their own way, so it is with the various contradictions that come out in a comparison of the accounts of the Real which are to be found in the various world religions.

Hick's view has proved attractive to many, and offers a solution to some of the difficulties with exclusivism. It fits well with, and indeed is motivated by, various ideas that are attractive to the modern mind: freedom of the individual to choose his or her own world-view; the rise of the scientific mind-set; the rejection of the literal truth of religious claims; the rise in moral relativism; the desire to be non-judgemental of others' beliefs. Yet it is a view which comes with serious problems of its own, problems that lead some to argue that it is not a plausible response to the problem of religious diversity. One problem is that it is often defended by appeal to an anti-realist epistemology, such as Kant's, or even by a scepticism about whether human beings can ever know the truth about anything in their experience. Although both of these epistemological positions are popular today in various academic disciplines (and consequently have found their way into popular culture), they are fraught with problems, and religious believers in particular, no matter what their denomination, are often loath to commit to them.

One problem facing the Kantian view is that it appears contradictory, for it is saying on the one hand that, as the elephant example clearly illustrates, there is no ultimate perspective from which we can judge which world religion might be true. On the other hand, Hick himself is taking an ultimate perspective, because he is giving us *a description of how things really are*! To put this another way, Hick is saying that the human mind cannot escape from the phenomenal world to describe what the noumenal world is like, and yet he is able to give us a supposedly true description (not one modified by the mind) of reality: that it consists of the noumenal and phenomenal worlds, and of a specific relationship between them. This is a contradiction at the heart of all anti-realist theories: the person proposing the theory is always able to escape from the relativising structures of the knowing mind that he is arguing nobody else can escape from! Pluralism also overtly flirts with scepticism about knowledge because it is based on the view that it is not possible to examine the world religions in the way the exclusivist argued for – to see which one is more likely to be true. It goes further than this by arguing that straightforward factual claims in the world's religions are all false, such as the claim that Jesus rose from the dead, or that the angel appeared to Mohammed, and are best understood as metaphors to express the Real. Therefore, the literalness of most religious claims – which is at the heart of nearly all religions – would have to be abandoned. So if a Christian were to think that Jesus was God, and really rose from the dead to save mankind, and that we should therefore pray to God, these beliefs should not be regarded as literally true beliefs, according to Hick, but as 'perspectives' on the Real, which in itself is unknowable. And it is the same with all religions. It is easy to see how such a view invites relativism and scepticism about religion in general, and would be hard to distinguish from atheism.

Pluralists will often reply to this criticism by saying that in religion what is important is not so much what you believe, but *how you live*, or as Hick puts it, what matters is that religion can transform one's life from being self-centred to being God-centred. If you follow the right moral code in your life, you will find favour in the eyes of God, irrespective of your metaphysical, theological and doctrinal beliefs (and so this pluralist approach would have room for secularists and atheists as well). This is a view that even those who are not pluralists have some sympathy for, but it would seem to require that we know what the right way to live *is* (that is, that we know what it means to live a God-centred life). But knowing what the right way to live is would seem to require that we be able to do two things that pluralists believe cannot be done. First, we would have to be able to judge the various religions *according to their moral codes*. But if we can do this for their moral codes, why can't we do it for their theological, sociological and historical features as well? Second, more generally, it would have to be possible for us *to know what the objective truth in morality is*, and if we can know the objective truth in morality, why can't we know it in other areas of knowledge, such as history, theology and accounts of revelation?

Pluralism, in short, is 'exclusivist' in its own way in that the pluralist wants both the exclusivist and the inclusivist to accept his view as true, and not just in general, but also with regard to what living a God-centred life *involves*. The pluralist believes he has the correct answer to this, and that other answers are incorrect.[6] In other words, in the elephant story, the pluralist is the sighted man who can see the whole picture, including the nature of the Real (the elephant), but everyone else is blind! If this were not the case, the pluralist could not know that the descriptions of the Real offered by the blind men were inadequate distortions. These problems are serious for pluralism, and have led many to propose a middle way between exclusivism and pluralism.

RELIGIOUS INCLUSIVISM

Many see the problems identified above in both exclusivism and pluralism as serious, and so they gravitate towards a view that would enable us to say both that salvation can be achieved in many different religions, but that nevertheless not all religions can be true. There may still only be one true religion. This view is known as religious inclusivism. Inclusivists hold that there is only one true account of how salvation can be achieved, but that people from different religions are saved because of the nature of this account of salvation. For example, a Christian inclusivist would hold that the death and resurrection of Jesus Christ makes salvation possible for all human beings, that this act makes salvation possible not just for Christians, but for members of other religions as well. This is true even if the members of the other religions do not recognize Jesus or Christianity; indeed, it is true even if they think Jesus was not God, or that the main claims of Christianity are false. The Catholic theologian Karl Rahner (1904–1984) and the Catholic philosopher Jacques Maritain (1882–1973) each held this view.[7]

This position, therefore, holds that salvation depends on a particular act – the death and resurrection of Jesus, for instance – being metaphysically true (it really occurred in history, and really had such and such an effect), but it is not necessary to *believe* that this event occurred, or even to be a member of the religion which holds the correct account of what had to happen for salvation to be (metaphysically) possible. What matters is that one lives a moral life, which it is possible to do in many different (not necessarily all) worldviews, and that one strives after a genuine relationship with God, who is revealed in many religions to some extent, even if imperfectly. The truth of the doctrinal beliefs of one's religion are of secondary importance. According to Christian inclusivists, it is the main facts of the Christian religion that make salvation possible, whether people recognize these facts or not. A Muslim or Jewish inclusivist would adopt exactly the same view with regard to the main claims of their respective religions.

Inclusivists argue that this is the most logical approach to the problem of religious diversity for several reasons. First, they agree with the exclusivist argument that logically all religions cannot be true. The inclusivist accepts this point but develops a view in which the debate about which religion is actually true is less pressing (unlike for exclusivists, where it is urgent). Second, this position also acknowledges the difficulty of deciding (with enough certainty to be an exclusivist) which of the world's religions is likely to be true based on historical, philosophical and theological arguments. Although this question is not irrelevant for the inclusivist (as it seems to be for the pluralist), it is not urgent that we settle it. Third, inclusivism is founded on the claim that there must be *some account of reality that is metaphysically and factually true* and that makes salvation possible. This seems to be a logical requirement of any religion, according to the inclusivist, and so inclusivism can preserve the philosophical and logical integrity of religious belief by refusing to accept the pluralist argument that religious claims, although seemingly literal, are in fact really metaphors.

We might use an analogy here to illustrate the inclusivist position. Suppose that in a particular city engineers put fluoride into the water, and that this leads to the people in the town having healthier teeth. The inclusivist holds that the fluoride really is in the water, and is really responsible for the healthier teeth. These facts are true not just for those who believe that there is fluoride in the water, and that it leads to healthier teeth, but even for all those who deny one or both of these facts. All that matters is that one drink the water! This is analogous to the way in which the Christian inclusivist thinks that the death and resurrection of Jesus makes salvation possible for all, as long as they live the right kind of life and genuinely seek out God. It does not matter whether they believe in Christianity, or whether they believe that Jesus lived but did not rise from the dead, or whatever. All that matters – metaphysically – is that Jesus did rise from the dead, and that this act made salvation possible for all, irrespective of one's particular religion.

Inclusivism is attractive to the modern mind, because it seems to preserve the strengths of both the other views, while avoiding their weaknesses. Yet it is not without its critics. Exclusivists criticize it on a number of grounds. First, they reject the view that we cannot investigate which world religion is likely to be true; second, they think that it demeans the philosophical integrity of a religion to claim that there need be no real or essential connection between the doctrinal and theological beliefs of the religion and its moral beliefs. Inclusivism, they claim, is hampered by the same problem as pluralism – it holds that in most world religions (except the correct one), the theological and doctrinal beliefs are false, but that the moral beliefs may not be particularly affected. But this view demeans one's beliefs, the exclusivist argues, from a logical point of view. In particular, it must inevitably lead to a weakening of the general position of religion in the debate with secularism, especially in the political arena. Pluralists are also not enthusiastic about inclusivism, because they have problems with the idea that we can work out which religion is true, which we would need to do if we are to be inclusivists, though they acknowledge the pragmatic value of inclusivism, in the sense that because the inclusivist believes that salvation is possible through many religions, the actual debate on which world religion is true is much less pressing, and therefore much less contentious.

Another difficulty for the inclusivist is that in order to say that people from other religions can be saved, one must provide some account of what salvation consists in if the inclusivist view is to have any content and is not to remain a vague, impractical abstraction. This will involve both a theological account of salvation, and some account of the correct moral life required for salvation. It will also require an argument that one does not need to believe the theological account in order to be saved, that living morally is sufficient and that God is revealed imperfectly in various religious traditions. Even if we cannot get agreement on the theological account, and, as we have noted, even if the theological debate is less urgent, the account of the correct way to live (the correct moral code) would seem to be urgent; otherwise we would quickly fall into moral relativism.

This means that the inclusivist must have a fairly detailed account of the correct moral way in which to live, and the problem with this, critics point out, is that it would seem to require that we have some perspective on which particular theological account of salvation is true after all, because surely the moral account is one that we must believe is part of God's plan for humanity. So in order to know the correct moral account, would we not also need to know the correct theological account? One way around this problem perhaps is to adopt a natural law approach, where we try to work out, on independent philosophical grounds (without appeal to a particular theological tradition), an account of the objectively right way to live. At least this way, all religions could communicate with each other on this crucial question. In short, the correct account of the right way to live is an important matter for the inclusivist position, and it may not be possible to produce such an account without first settling the matter of which world religion is true, which would be a fatal blow to the inclusivist project.

The question of the status of missionary work is an interesting one for inclusivists, and they have struggled with it in the modern world. On the one hand, missionary work would not seem to be quite so important since people in all religions can be saved. On the other hand, surely one would want people to convert to, and to believe, the true religion if at all possible, and this fact might still prompt the inclusivist to support missionary work. The general tendency of inclusivists has been to downplay missionary work, and to stress the positive points of other religions.

In conclusion, let us not forget that some missionary work is required by all of the views we have covered in this chapter, because their proponents have to convert others to what they regard as the correct position on the matter of religious diversity and, as we have seen above, this task seems to require that one knows what the truth is on religious matters, at least to some degree. This latter point illustrates yet again why the problem of religious pluralism is a fascinating, but complex, matter for the various religions in the modern world.

NOTES

CHAPTER 1

1   For these and other possible definitions of religion, see Irving Hexham, *Concise Dictionary of Religion* (Downer's Grove, IL: InterVarsity Press, 1993).

CHAPTER 2

1   Among Arabic philosophers who discussed the argument were al-Kindi (c. 801–873) and al-Ghazali (1058–1111).
2   For the Bonaventure/Thomas debate, see Cyril Vollert *et al.* (eds), *St. Thomas Aquinas, Siger of Brabant, St. Bonaventure: On the Eternity of the World* (Milwaukee: Marquette University Press, 1964).
3   See William L. Craig, *The Kalām Cosmological Argument* (Eugene, OR: Wipf and Stock, 1979); also his essay 'Philosophical and Scientific Pointers to *Creatio ex Nihilo*', in R. Douglas Geivett and Brendan Sweetman (eds), *Contemporary Perspectives on Religious Epistemology* (New York: Oxford University Press, 1992), pp. 185–200.
4   For a good overview of the Big Bang theory, and scientific work on the origin of the universe in general, see Stephen Hawking, *A Brief History of Time* (New York: Bantam, 1988).
5   See Paul Edwards, 'A Critique of the Cosmological Argument', in L. Pojman (ed.), *Philosophy of Religion: An Anthology* (Belmont, CA: Wadsworth, 2003), pp. 59–73; also see Michael Martin, *Atheism: A Philosophical Justification* (Philadelphia: Temple University Press, 1990), pp. 97–104.
6   See Paul Draper, 'A Critique of the Kalam Cosmological Argument', in Pojman (ed.), *Philosophy of Religion*, pp. 42–47.
7   Quintin Smith, 'Infinity and the Past', in W.L. Craig and Q. Smith (eds), *Theism, Atheism and Big Bang Cosmology* (Oxford: Clarendon Press, 1993), p. 96.

8 William L. Craig, 'Time and Infinity,' *ibid.*, pp. 96–97.
9 William L. Craig, 'Philosophical and Scientific Pointers to Creatio ex Nihilo,' in Geivett and Sweetman (eds), *Contemporary Perspectives*, p. 196.
10 See St Thomas Aquinas, *Summa Theologica*, Part 1, Question 2, Article 3, in Anton Pegis (ed.), *Introduction to St. Thomas Aquinas* (New York: Random House, 1945), pp. 24–27; see also *Summa Contra Gentiles*, Part 1, chapters 9–14, in Ralph McInerny (ed.), *Thomas Aquinas: Selected Writings* (Harmondsworth: Penguin, 1998), pp. 243–256.
11 Thomas Aquinas, *Summa Theologica*, Part 1, Question 2, Article 3, in Pegis (ed.), *Introduction to St. Thomas Aquinas*, pp. 25–6.
12 See Frederick Copleston, *Aquinas* (Harmondsworth: Pelican, 1975), pp. 121ff.
13 See Dallas Willard, 'The Three-Stage Argument for the Existence of God', in Geivett and Sweetman (eds), *Contemporary Perspectives*, p. 214.
14 Richard Taylor, *Metaphysics* (Englewood Cliffs, NJ: Prentice Hall, 1963), p. 93.
15 See Russell's famous debate with Copleston on the existence of God, in Bertrand Russell, *Why I Am Not a Christian* (London: George Allen & Unwin, 1957), pp. 133–153.
16 William Rowe, *Philosophy of Religion* (Belmont, CA: Wadsworth, 2001, third edn), pp. 26–28.
17 See William Paley, *Natural Theology* (New York: Oxford University Press, 2006).
18 Dallas Willard, 'The Three-Stage Argument for the Existence of God', in Geivett and Sweetman (eds), *Contemporary Perspectives*, p. 219.
19 Richard Swinburne, *The Existence of God* (Oxford: Clarendon Press, 1991), pp. 138–139.
20 Charles Taliaferro, *Contemporary Philosophy of Religion* (New York: Blackwell, 1998), p. 365.
21 See Richard Swinburne, 'The Argument from Design', in Geivett and Sweetman (eds), *Contemporary Perspectives*, pp. 201–211.
22 See Stephen J. Gould, *Wonderful Life: The Burgess Shale and the Nature of History* (New York: Norton, 1990).
23 Richard Dawkins, *The Blind Watchmaker* (New York: Norton, 1987), p. 6.
24 See Hawking, *A Brief History of Time*, p. 121, p. 125.
25 Martin, *Atheism*, p. 133.
26 J.J.C. Smart and J.J. Haldane, *Atheism and Theism* (Oxford: Blackwell, 1996), p. 18.

CHAPTER 3

1 Anselm, *Proslogion* (trans and ed. Max Charlesworth), *St. Anselm's Proslogion* (Oxford: Clarendon Press, 1965), p. 115.
2 *Ibid.*, p. 103.
3 Anselm, *Proslogion* (trans. by A.C. McGill), in John Hick and A.C. McGill (eds), *The Many-Faced Argument* (New York: Macmillan, 1967),

p. 4. This volume also includes Gaunilo's *Reply on Behalf of the Fool*, Anselm's *Reply* to Gaunilo, as well as many contemporary essays on the argument.

4 *Ibid.*, p. 5.

5 Gaunilo's *Reply on Behalf of the Fool*, in Charlesworth (ed.), p. 23.

6 Immanuel Kant, *Critique of Pure Reason*, trans. N.K. Smith (London: Macmillan), p. 505.

7 See Norman Malcolm, 'Anselm's Ontological Arguments', in Hick and McGill (eds), *The Many-Faced Argument*, pp. 301–321.

8 See Hick and McGill (eds), *The Many-Faced Argument*, pp. 341–356.

9 Malcolm, 'Anselm's Ontological Arguments', in *The Many-Faced Argument*, p. 312.

10 See Charles Hartshorne, 'The Necessarily Existent', in Alvin Plantinga (ed.), *The Ontological Argument* (New York: Doubleday, 1965), pp. 123–35.

11 See also on this matter, Thomas Morris, *Anselmian Reflections: Essays in Philosophical Theology* (Notre Dame, IN: Notre Dame University Press, 1987).

12 Kant, *Critique of Pure Reason*, trans. Smith, p. 502.

13 See Immanuel Kant, *Critique of Practical Reason*, trans. W.S. Pluhar (Indianapolis, IN: Hackett, 2002), p. 115.

14 *Ibid.*, p. 158.

15 See C.S. Lewis, *Mere Christianity* (San Francisco: HarperSanFrancisco, 2001), Book 1.

16 Charles Taliaferro, *Contemporary Philosophy of Religion* (Malden, MA: Blackwell, 1998), p. 370.

17 See Hume's essay, 'Of Miracles', in his *Enquiry Concerning Human Understanding*, trans. L.A. Selby-Bigge (London: Oxford University Press, 1902).

18 See R.F. Holland, 'The Miraculous', in Richard Swinburne (ed.), *Miracles* (New York: Prentice Hall, 1989).

19 As an example, see Stephen T. Davies, *Risen Indeed: Making Sense of the Resurrection* (Grand Rapids, MI: Eerdmans, 1993).

20 See Michael Martin, *The Case against Christianity* (Philadelphia, PA: Temple University Press, 1991), ch. 3, esp. p. 96ff.

21 See Alvin Plantinga, 'Is theism really a miracle?', *Faith & Philosophy* (1986) vol. 3, pp. 109–134.

CHAPTER 4

1 There are many fine books on the general topic of God's nature. Here is a sample: Thomas V. Morris, *Our Idea of God* (Notre Dame, IN: University of Notre Dame Press, 1991); Richard Swinburne, *The Coherence of Theism* (Oxford: Clarendon Press, 1986); William Alston, *Divine Nature and Human Language* (Ithaca, NY: Cornell University Press, 1989); David Burrell, *Knowing the Unknowable God: Ibn-Sina, Maimonides, Aquinas* (Notre Dame, IN: University of Notre Dame

Press, 1986); Stephen T. Davies, *Logic and the Nature of God* (New York: Macmillan, 1983); Richard Gale, *On the Nature and Existence of God* (Cambridge: Cambridge University Press, 1991); Ronald H. Nash, *The Concept of God* (Grand Rapids, MI: Zondervan, 1983).

2 For more on analogy as it applies to God's nature, see Ralph McInerny, *Aquinas and Analogy* (Washington, DC: Catholic University of America Press, 1998).

3 See Thomas Aquinas, *Summa Theologica*, Part 1, Questions 3–25 (New York: Benziger Brothers, 1947), pp. 14–141.

4 For an excellent discussion of St Thomas's views on this and other matters, see Brian Davies, *The Thought of Thomas Aquinas* (Oxford: Clarendon Press, 1992).

5 See Swinburne, *The Coherence of Theism*; and Alvin Plantinga, *Does God have a Nature?* (Milwaukee: Marquette University Press,1980).

6 See Charles Hartshorne, *Omnipotence and Other Theological Mistakes* (New York: State University of New York Press, 1983); see also John B. Cobb and David Ray Griffin, *Process Theology: An Introductory Exposition* (Philadelphia: Westminister Press, 1976).

7 See Richard Swinburne, *Is there a God?* (New York: Oxford University Press, 1996), p. 45.

8 For more on views of God in the Bible, see J.N.D. Kelly, *Early Christian Doctrines* (London: Continuum, 2000).

9 See Thomas Aquinas, 'How the Omnipotent God is Said to be Incapable of Certain Things', in Eleonore Stump and Michael J. Murray (eds), *Philosophy of Religion: The Big Questions* (Malden, MA: Blackwell, 1999), pp. 7–9.

10 *Ibid.*, p. 8.

11 Samuel Clarke, *Works: British Philosophers and Theologians of the 17th and 18th Centuries* (New York: Garland Press, 1978), vol. IV, p. 717.

12 For more on this paradox, see the articles in Alfred Freddoso (ed.), *The Existence and Nature of God* (Notre Dame, IN: University of Notre Dame Press, 1983); and Richard Swinburne, *The Coherence of Theism*, ch. 9.

13 For a good statement of this view, see Augustine, *The Confessions* (New York: Oxford, 1998), Book 11.

14 For more on the Hindu view of God, see Huston Smith, *The World's Religions* (San Francisco: HarperSanFrancisco, 1991), ch. 2.

CHAPTER 5

1 David Hume, *Dialogues Concerning Natural Religion* (New York: Bobbs-Merrill, 1947), p. 198. For a classic response to the problem of evil, see G.W. Leibniz, *Theodicy*, ed. A. Farrer (New Haven: Yale University Press, 1952).

2 See J.L. Mackie, 'Evil and Omnipotence', in Marilyn McCord Adams and Robert Adams (eds), *The Problem of Evil* (New York: Oxford

University Press), pp. 25–27; see also Mackie, *The Miracle of Theism*, ch. 9, for a modification of his view.

3 See William Rowe, 'The Problem of Evil and Some Varieties of Atheism', in R. Douglas Geivett and Brendan Sweetman (eds), *Contemporary Perspectives on Religious Epistemology* (New York: Oxford University Press), pp. 33–42.

4 See Alvin Plantinga, *God, Freedom and Evil* (Grand Rapids, MI: Eerdmans, 1976), part 1; see also Michael Peterson, *Evil and the Christian God* (Grand Rapids, MI: Baker, 1982), p. 103. For other excellent studies of the general problem of evil, see Michael Peterson, *God and Evil: An Introduction to the Issues* (Boulder, CO: Westview, 1988); James Petrik, *Evil Beyond Belief* (Armonk, NY: M.E. Sharpe, 2000); R. Douglas Geivett, *Evil and the Evidence for God* (Philadelphia, PA: Temple University Press, 1993).

5 See C.S. Lewis's reflections on the problem of evil in his *The Problem of Pain* (New York: Macmillan, 1962).

6 See St Augustine, *City of God*, trans. Henry Bettenson (Middlesex: Penguin, 1972), xii, sections 6–7; see also his *Enchiridion* (Washington, DC: Gateway Editions, 1996), section 8.

7 See Alvin Plantinga, *The Nature of Necessity* (Oxford: Clarendon, 1974), pp. 191ff.; also reprinted as 'God, Evil and the Metaphysics of Freedom', in Adams and Adams (eds), *The Problem of Evil*, pp. 83–109.

8 See William Alston, 'The Inductive Argument from Evil and the Human Cognitive Condition', in Daniel Howard-Synder (eds), *The Evidential Argument from Evil* (Bloomington, IN: Indiana UP, 1996), pp. 97–125.

9 John Hick, *Evil and the God of Love* (New York: Harper and Row, 1966), p. 361.

10 John Hick, 'An Irenaean Theodicy', in Stephen T. Davis (ed.), *Encountering Evil: Live Options in Theodicy* (Atlanta, GA: John Knox Press, 1981), p. 44.

11 *Ibid.*, p. 52.

12 C.S. Lewis, *The Problem of Pain*, p. 32. See also David Basinger, 'Evil as Evidence against God's Existence', in Michael Peterson (ed.), *The Problem of Evil* (Notre Dame, IN: University of Notre Dame, 1992), pp. 177ff.

13 See Richard Swinburne, 'Some Major Strands of Theodicy', in Daniel Howard-Synder (eds), *The Evidential Argument from Evil*, pp. 30–48; also Eleonore Stump, 'Aquinas on the Sufferings of Job', in the same volume, pp. 49–68.

14 H.J. McCloskey, 'God and Evil', *Philosophical Quarterly*, vol. 10 (1960), pp. 97–114.

CHAPTER 6

1 St John of the Cross, Stanza II of *Living Flame of Love* in St John of the Cross, *Collected Works*, trans. K. Kavanaugh, O.C.D. and Otilio Rodriquez, O.C.D. (Washington, DC: ICS, 1991), p. 664.

2 *The Life of Teresa of Jesus*, ed. and trans. E. Allison Peers (New York: Doubleday, 1960), p. 249.

3 See Rudolf Otto, *The Idea of the Holy* (Oxford: Oxford University Press, 1958).

4 For an example of another fideistic view that differs from reformed epistemology and that, in addition to denying that belief in God requires evidence, also offers a radical reinterpretation of religious language and meaning, see D.Z. Phillips, *Faith and Philosophical Enquiry* (London: Routledge, 1970); and *Faith after Foundationalism* (Boulder, CO: Westview, 1988).

5 See Alvin Plantinga, 'Is Belief in God Properly Basic?', in R. Douglas Geivett and Brendan Sweetman (eds), *Contemporary Perspectives on Religious Epistemology* (Oxford: Oxford University Press, 1992), pp. 133–141; also A. Plantinga and N. Wolterstorff (eds), *Faith and Rationality: Reason and Belief in God* (Notre Dame, IN: University of Notre Dame Press, 1983).

6 Plantinga, 'Is Belief in God Properly Basic?,' in Geivett and Sweetman (eds), *Contemporary Perspectives*, p. 135.

7 For some critical reflections on Plantinga's and Alston's views, see Stewart Goetz, 'Belief in God Is Not Properly Basic', in Geivett and Sweetman (eds), *Contemporary Perspectives*, pp. 168–177; also Phillip Quinn, 'In Search of the Foundations of Theism', *Faith and Philosophy*, 2 (1985), pp. 469–486; and Richard Gale, *On the Nature and Existence of God* (Cambridge: Cambridge University Press, 1991), ch. 8.

8 See William Alston, 'Religious Experience and Religious Belief', in Geivett and Sweetman (eds), *Contemporary Perspectives*, pp. 295–303; and also his *Perceiving God* (Ithaca, NY: Cornell University Press, 1991).

9 Plantinga, 'Is Belief In God Properly Basic?,' in Geivett and Sweetman (eds), *Contemporary Perspectives*, p. 140.

10 See Wayne Proudfoot, *Religious Experience* (Berkeley, CA: University of California Press, 1985).

11 See 'The Rationality of Religious Belief', in Geivett and Sweetman (eds), *Contemporary Perspectives*, pp. 304–319; see also his *An Interpretation of Religion: Human Responses to the Transcendent* (London: Macmillan, 1989).

12 See Nelson Pike, *Mystic Union* (Ithaca, NY: Cornell University Press, 1992), p. 32, where he says that this type of experience is where 'God is experienced as a not-me that stands in contrast to the experiencing subject'.

13 See Richard Swinburne, *The Existence of God* (Oxford: Clarendon Press, 1991), pp. 254ff.

CHAPTER 7

1 See Richard Blackwell, *Science, Religion and Authority: Lessons from the Galileo Affair* (Milwaukee: Marquette University Press, 1998). I am indebted to Professor Blackwell's excellent study of science and religion

for my exposition of St Augustine's and Galileo's views in the first part of this chapter.

2   *Ibid.*, p. 25.
3   See Stanley L. Jaki, *The Road of Science and the Ways to God* (Chicago: University of Chicago Press, 1978).
4   Some representative works include: Francis Crick, *The Astonishing Hypothesis* (New York: Touchstone, 1995); Carl Sagan, *Cosmos* (New York: Random House, 1983); Steven Weinberg, *Dreams of a Final Theory* (New York: Pantheon, 1992); and Richard Dawkins, *The Blind Watchmaker: Why the Evidence of Evolution Reveals a Universe Without Design* (New York: Norton, 1987).
5   Evolution can be a difficult topic. One very good introductory overview of the main outlines of the theory is: Carl Zimmer, *Evolution* (New York: HarperCollins, 2001); see also, Ernst Mayr, *What Evolution Is* (New York: Basic Books, 2002), and Stephen J. Gould, *Wonderful Life: The Burgess Shale and the Nature of History* (New York: Norton, 1990).
6   See Michael Behe, *Darwin's Black Box* (New York: Free Press, 1996); William Dembski, *Intelligent Design* (Downer's Grove, IL: InterVarsity, 1999). For criticisms of ID theory, see Kenneth Miller, *Finding Darwin's God* (New York: HarperCollins, 1999); and the debate in William Dembski and Michael Ruse (eds), *Debating Design: From Darwin to DNA* (Cambridge: Cambridge University Press, 2004).
7   See Philip Johnson, *Darwin on Trial* (Downer's Grove, IL: InterVarsity, 1993); for a critique of Johnson see Miller's book above.
8   For further excellent discussions of the relationship between religion and science, see Ian Barbour, *Religion and Science* (San Francisco: HarperCollins, 1997 rev.ed.); and John Haught, *Responses to 101 Questions on God and Evolution* (New Jersey: Paulist Press, 2001).
9   For more on the topics discussed in this section, see Eric Matthews, *Mind: Key Concepts in Philosophy* (London: Continuum, 2005); E. J. Lowe, *An Introduction to the Philosophy of Mind* (Cambridge: Cambridge University Press, 2000); Stanley Jaki, *Minds, Brains and Computers* (New York: Regnery, 1989); John Searle, *Minds, Brains and Science* (Cambridge, MA: Harvard University Press, 1986); John Heil (ed.), *Philosophy of Mind: A Guide and Anthology* (New York: Oxford, 2004); Ric Machuga, *In Defense of the Soul* (Grand Rapids, MI: Brazos Press, 2002); and Paul Edwards (ed.), *Immortality* (Amherst, N.Y.: Prometheus Books, 1997).

CHAPTER 8

1   For excellent introductions to the issues raised by the problem of religious pluralism, see Mortimer Adler, *Truth in Religion* (New York: Macmillan, 1990); John Hick, *God and the Universe of Faiths* (London: Macmillan, 1977); S. Mark Heim, *Salvations: Truth and Difference in Religion* (Maryknoll, NY: Orbis Books, 1995); and Phillip L. Quinn and

Kevin Meeker (eds), *The Philosophical Challenge of Religious Diversity* (New York: Oxford University Press, 2000).

2 See Karl Barth, *Church Dogmatics,* Vol. 1 (Edinburgh: T & T Clark, 1956).

3 See Dennis L. Okholm and Timothy R. Phillips (eds), *Four Views on Salvation in a Pluralist World* (Grand Rapids, MI: Zondervan, 1996).

4 For a discussion of the logic of exclusivism, see Alvin Plantinga, 'A Defense of Religious Exclusivism', in Phillip L. Quinn and Kevin Meeker (eds), *The Philosophical Challenge of Religious Diversity*, pp. 172–192.

5 See John Hick, *God and the Universe of Faiths* (London: Macmillan, 1977).

6 See Peter Byrne, 'A Religious Theory of Religion', *Religious Studies*, vol. 27 (1991), pp. 121–132; also his *Prolegomena to Religious Pluralism* (Basingstoke: Palgrave Macmillan, 1995).

7 See Jacques Maritain, *The Degrees of Knowledge*, trans. G. Phelan (New York: Charles Scribner's Sons, 1959); Karl Rahner, 'Christians and the Non-Christian Religions', in John Hick and Brian Hebblethwaite (eds), *Christianity and Other Religions* (Oxford: OneWorld, 2001), pp. 19–38.

GUIDE TO FURTHER READING

Adams, Marilyn McCord and Robert Adams (eds), *The Problem of Evil* (New York: Oxford University Press, 1990).

Adler, Mortimer, *Truth in Religion* (New York: Macmillan, 1990).

Augustine, St, *The Confessions* (New York: Oxford, 1998).

Barbour, Ian, *Religion and Science* (San Francisco: HarperCollins, 1997 rev. edn).

Behe, Michael, *Darwin's Black Box* (New York: Free Press, 1996).

Blackwell, Richard, *Science, Religion and Authority: Lessons from the Galileo Affair* (Milwaukee: Marquette University Press, 1998).

Cahn, Steven and David Shatz, *Questions about God: Today's Philosophers Ponder the Divine* (New York: Oxford University Press, 2002).

Cobb and David Ray Griffin, *Process Theology: An Introductory Exposition* (Philadelphia: Westminister Press, 1976).

Copleston, Frederick, *Aquinas* (Harmondsworth: Pelican, 1975).

Craig, William, L., *The Kalām Cosmological Argument* (Eugene, OR: Wipf and Stock, 1979).

—— and Q. Smith, *Theism, Atheism and Big Bang Cosmology* (Oxford: Clarendon Press, 1993).

Davies, Brian, *The Thought of Thomas Aquinas* (Oxford: Clarendon Press, 1992).

Davies, Stephen, T., *Risen Indeed: Making Sense of the Resurrection* (Grand Rapids, MI: Eerdmans, 1993).

Dawkins, Richard, *The Blind Watchmaker* (New York: Norton, 1987).

Dembski, William, *Intelligent Design* (Downer's Grove, IL: InterVarsity, 1999).

Freddoso, Aldred (ed.), *The Existence and Nature of God* (Notre Dame, IN: University of Notre Dame Press, 1983).

Gale, Richard, *On the Nature and Existence of God* (Cambridge: Cambridge University Press, 1991).

Geivett, R. Douglas, *Evil and the Evidence for God* (Philadelphia, PA: Temple University Press, 1993).

—— and Brendan Sweetman (eds), *Contemporary Perspectives on Religious Epistemology* (New York: Oxford University Press, 1992).

Green, Joel B. and Stuart L. Palmer (eds), *In Search of the Soul: Four Views of the Body–Mind Problem* (Downer's Grove, IL: InterVarsity, 2005).

Hancock, Curtis L. and Brendan Sweetman (eds), *Faith and the Life of the Intellect* (Washington, DC: Catholic University of America Press, 2003).

Hartshorne, Charles, *Omnipotence and Other Theological Mistakes* (New York: State University of New York Press, 1983).

Heim, S. Mark, *Salvations: Truth and Difference in Religion* (Maryknoll, NY: Orbis Books, 1995).

Hick, John, *An Interpretation of Religion: Human Responses to the Transcendent* (London: Macmillan, 1989).

—— *Evil and the God of Love* (New York: Harper and Row, 1966).

—— *God and the Universe of Faiths* (London: Macmillan, 1977).

—— and A.C. McGill (eds), *The Many-Faced Argument* (New York: Macmillan, 1967).

Hume, David, *Dialogues Concerning Natural Religion* (New York: Bobbs-Merrill, 1947).

Jaki, Stanley, L., *The Road of Science and the Ways to God* (Chicago: University of Chicago Press, 1978).

Lewis, C.S., *The Problem of Pain* (New York: Macmillan, 1962).

Machuga, Ric, *In Defense of the Soul* (Grand Rapids, MI: Brazos Press, 2002).

Mackie, John, *The Miracle of Theism* (Oxford: Oxford University Press, 1982).

Martin, Michael, *Atheism: A Philosophical Justification* (Philadelphia: Temple University Press, 1990).

McInerny, Ralph (ed.), *Thomas Aquinas: Selected Writings* (Harmondsworth: Penguin, 1998).

Miller, Kenneth, *Finding Darwin's God* (New York: HarperCollins, 1999).

Morris, Thomas, *Our Idea of God* (Notre Dame, IN: University of Notre Dame Press, 1991).

Okholm, Dennis L. and Timothy R. Phillips (eds), *Four Views on Salvation in a Pluralist World* (Grand Rapids, MI: Zondervan, 1996).

Otto, Rudolf, *The Idea of the Holy* (Oxford: Oxford University Press, 1958).

Petrik, James, *Evil Beyond Belief* (Armonk, NY: M.E. Sharpe, 2000).

Phillips, D.Z., *Faith and Philosophical Enquiry* (London: Routledge, 1970).

Pike, Nelson, *Mystic Union* (Ithaca, NY: Cornell University Press, 1992).

Plantinga, *God, Freedom, and Evil* (Grand Rapids, MI: Eerdmans, 1976).

—— and N. Wolterstorff (eds), *Faith and Rationality: Reason and Belief in God* (Notre Dame, IN: University of Notre Dame Press, 1983).

Proudfoot, Wayne, *Religious Experience* (Berkeley, CA: University of California Press, 1985).

Quinn, Phillip, and Kevin Meeker (eds), *The Philosophical Challenge of Religious Diversity* (New York: Oxford University Press, 2000).

—— and Charles Taliaferro (eds), *A Companion to Philosophy of Religion* (Oxford: Blackwell, 1999).

Sagan, Carl, *Cosmos* (New York: Random House, 1983).

Searle, John, *Minds, Brains and Science* (Cambridge, MA: Harvard University Press, 1986).

Smart, J.J.C. and J.J. Haldane, *Atheism and Theism* (Oxford: Blackwell, 1996).

Smith, Huston, *The World's Religions* (San Francisco: HarperSanFrancisco, 1991).

Stump, Eleonore and Michael Murray (eds), *Philosophy of Religion: The Big Questions* (Oxford: Blackwell, 1999).

Swinburne, Richard, *The Existence of God* (Oxford: Clarendon Press, 1991).

—— *Is there a God?* (New York: Oxford University Press, 1996).

—— *The Coherence of Theism* (Oxford: Clarendon Press, 1986).

—— (ed.), *Miracles* (New York: Prentice Hall, 1989).

Taliaferro, Charles, *Contemporary Philosophy of Religion* (New York: Blackwell, 1998).

Zagzebski, Linda, *The Dilemma of Freedom and Foreknowledge* (New York: Oxford University Press, 1996).

Zimmer, Carl, *Evolution* (New York: HarperCollins, 2001).

INDEX